compact houses

Edition 2005

Author: Carles Broto
Publisher: Arian Mostaedi
Editorial Coordinator: Jacobo Krauel
Architectural Advisor: Pilar Chueca
Graphic designer & production: Pilar Chueca, Marta Rojals
Text: contributed by the architects, edited by Núria Rodríguez

Jonqueres, 10, 1-5
08003 Barcelona, Spain
Tel.: +34 93 301 21 99
Fax: +34-93-301 00 21
E-mail: info@linksbooks.net
www. linksbooks.net

Printed in Spain

compact houses

INTRODUCTION

Architecture is the discipline that deals with space: it works in space, from and with space. From an architectural point of view, this conditioning element is becoming increasingly scarce and, paradoxically, the scarcer it is the more important its role in a project. The organization and optimization of space reveal an architect's skill in response to the challenges of a limited space, a small site or a reduced budget. In this sense, architecture has been able to reinvent itself over and over, through the new construction and technological advances that appear on an almost daily basis. The idea of the primitive "refuge", present at the gestation period of all smaller housing projects, leads into infinite dwelling possibilities that transcend the actual space and area available. Spatial optimization expands into the fields of versatility and the multifunctionality of constructive elements, including furnishings and installations.

Compact Houses provides a sampling of this ongoing architectural redefinition: an overview of urban, rural, transformable, demountable, transportable, traditional and experimental, weekend and permanent, houses. In all their manifestations, they show that in architecture, reduced and compact doesn't necessarily mean 'limited'.

This extensively documented book presents complete detailed technical and graphic information for each project and its design process, from conception to completion. The internationally recognized architects contribute additional information and details of the solutions adopted in each case. This combination provides a wide range of suggestions and useful examples that can help to define future projects. In short, an invaluable tool for all kinds of professionals and students of architecture and interior and furniture design.

Bauart Architekten

Small House / Option

Bern, Switzerland

This house, the result of a collaborative process between architects and manufacturers of prefabricated houses, constitutes a discreet and optimized habitation cell. Constructed entirely form wood, it was designed to produce maximum quality at minimum cost.

The totally prefabricated perimeter elements were pre-assembled in the workshop, forming two regular geometric shapes that were then transported to the site and erected on-site. The house can be assembled in a single day on 10 x 4 meter foundations

Four large windows, placed on each side of the building, allow different aspects of the surrounding landscape to enter the house, and create a generous interior space. An opening on the ground floor blurs the distinction between inside and outside space.

The 66 m^2 internal space is distributed over two levels. The modular construction means that the surface materials and furnishings can be adapted in many different ways to suit the needs and taste of the client.

By placing the functional nucleus of technical installations and the stairwell in the center, the space taken up for circulation is minimized and the living space is maximized. Although the house is small, the open plan and large windows create the feeling of living in a large space.

Photographs: Bauart Architekten

This prefabricated house can be adapted to different uses: as an addition to an existing building, as a continuous or L-shaped building, or as twin houses with an internal patio. It can also be used as an extension to an existing house, as a holiday house, studio, or home office space.

Ground floor plan

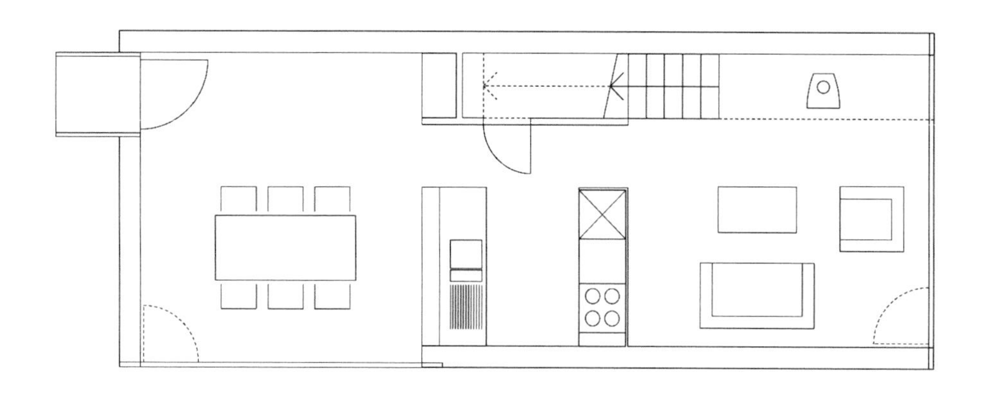

First floor plan

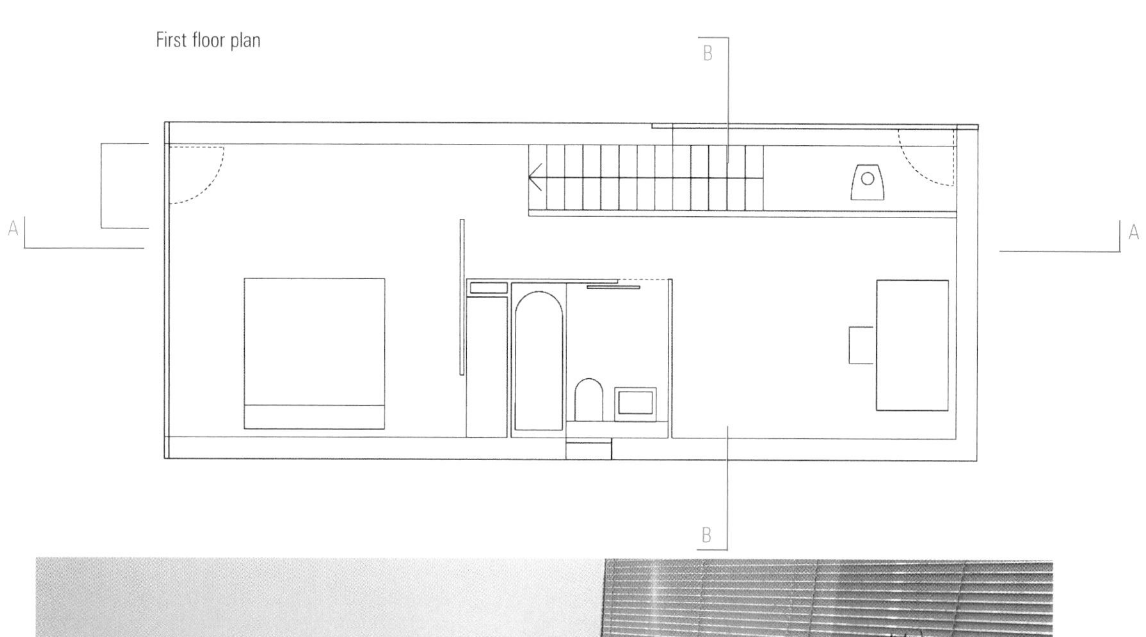

B2

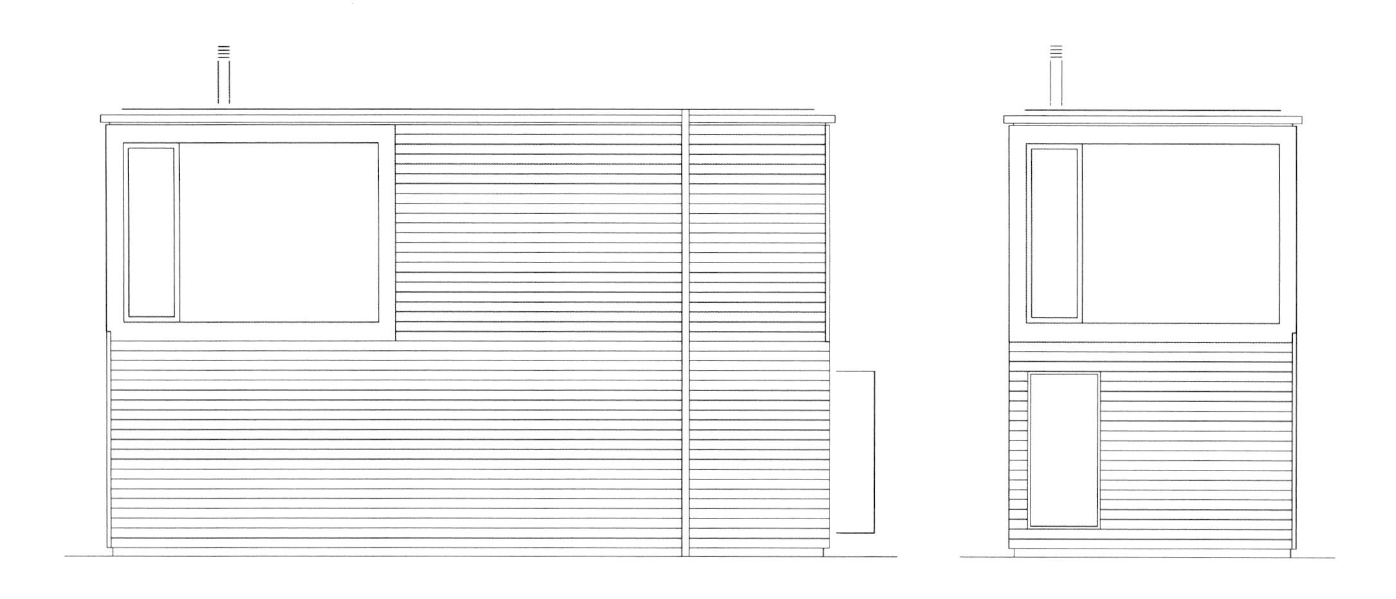

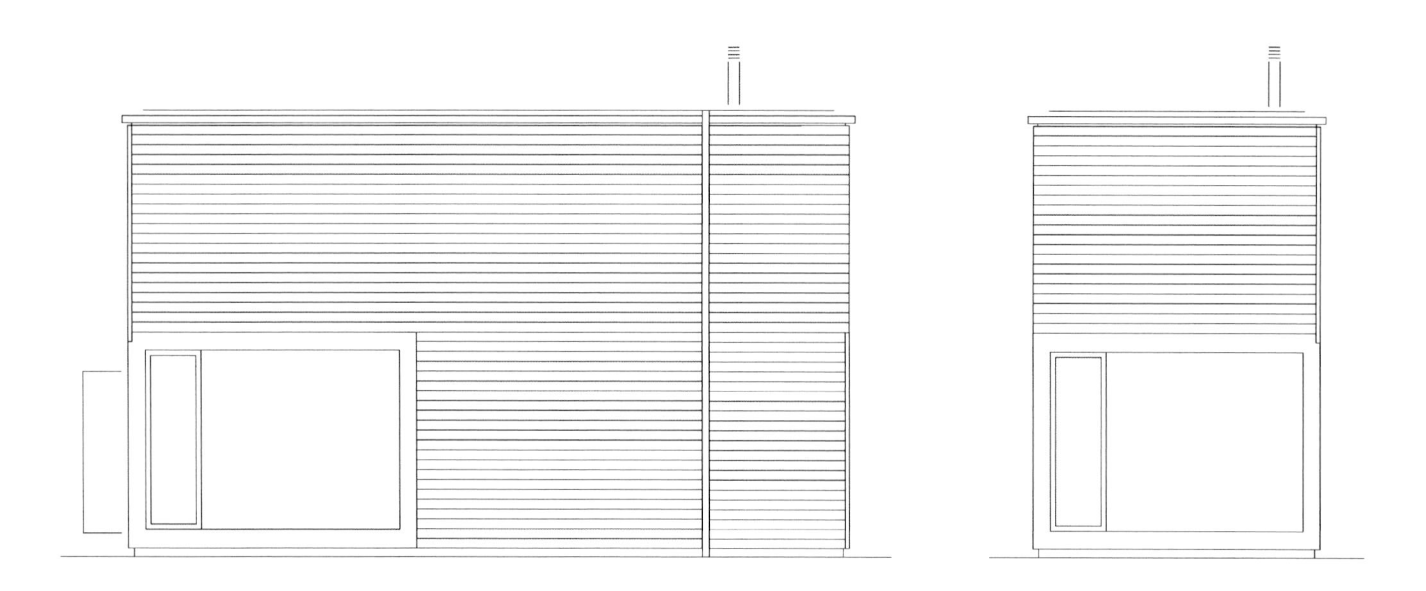

Elevations

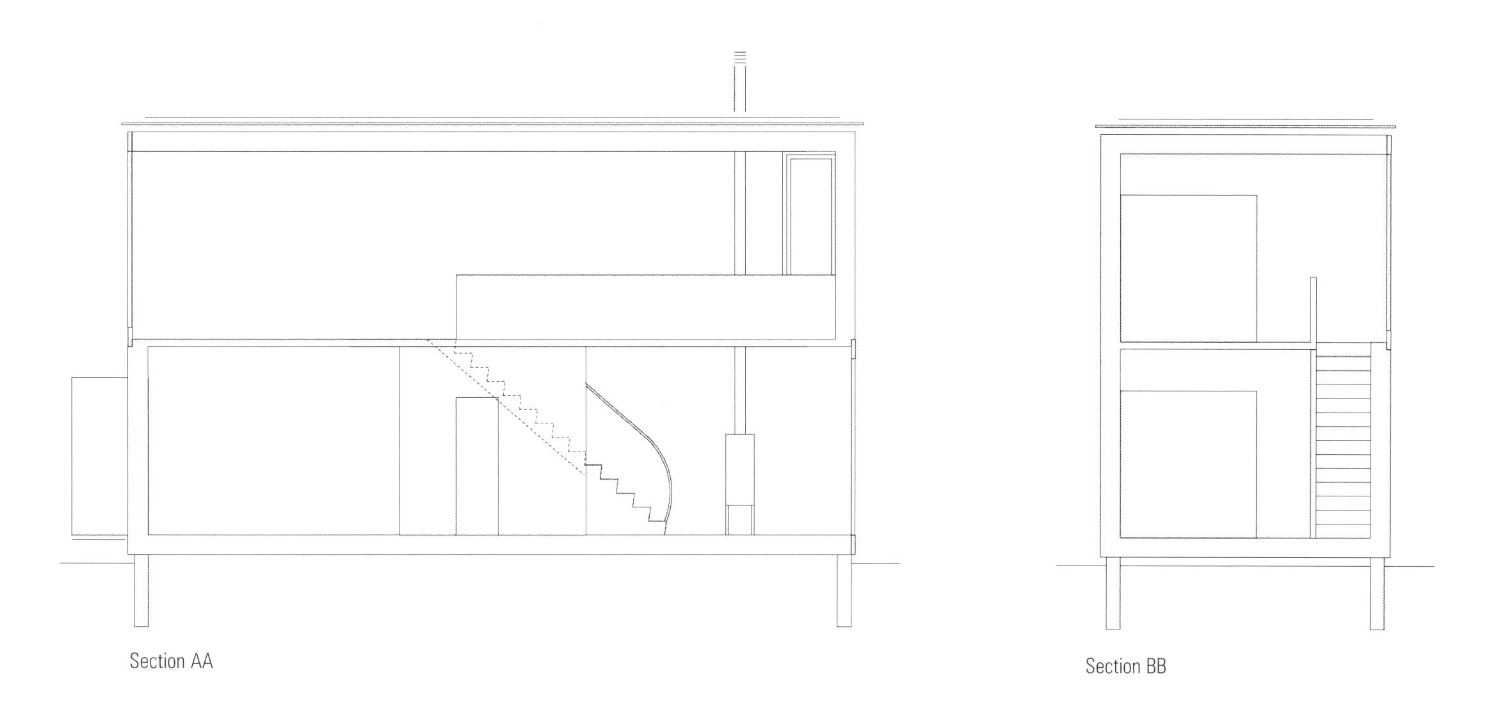
Section AA
Section BB

Bems Architektengemeinschaft Böwer Eith Murken

Haus Kaiser

Freiburg-Kappel, Germany

This detached house for a family with three children makes the most of the opportunities for "second row" building in an existing context. Surrounded by traditional double-pitched dwellings in Freiburg, the house is based on a clearly defied box shape with red timber cladding that makes maximum use of the site and accommodates all of the family's needs.

All windows open from floor to ceiling, allowing natural light into the space. The windows are arranged so as to ensure privacy while still commanding views over the picturesque Schauinsland mountain.

The ground floor is organized as an open plan with a kitchen, dining and living area and working space. Sliding doors separate the living space from the adjoining rooms. The bedrooms and the family bathroom are located on the upper floor.

The internal ambience is dominated by high-quality exposed concrete in combination with cherry timber flooring. The freestanding kitchen block is also made from exposed concrete that has been sanded, polished and waxed.

Photographs: Roland Halbe / ARTUR

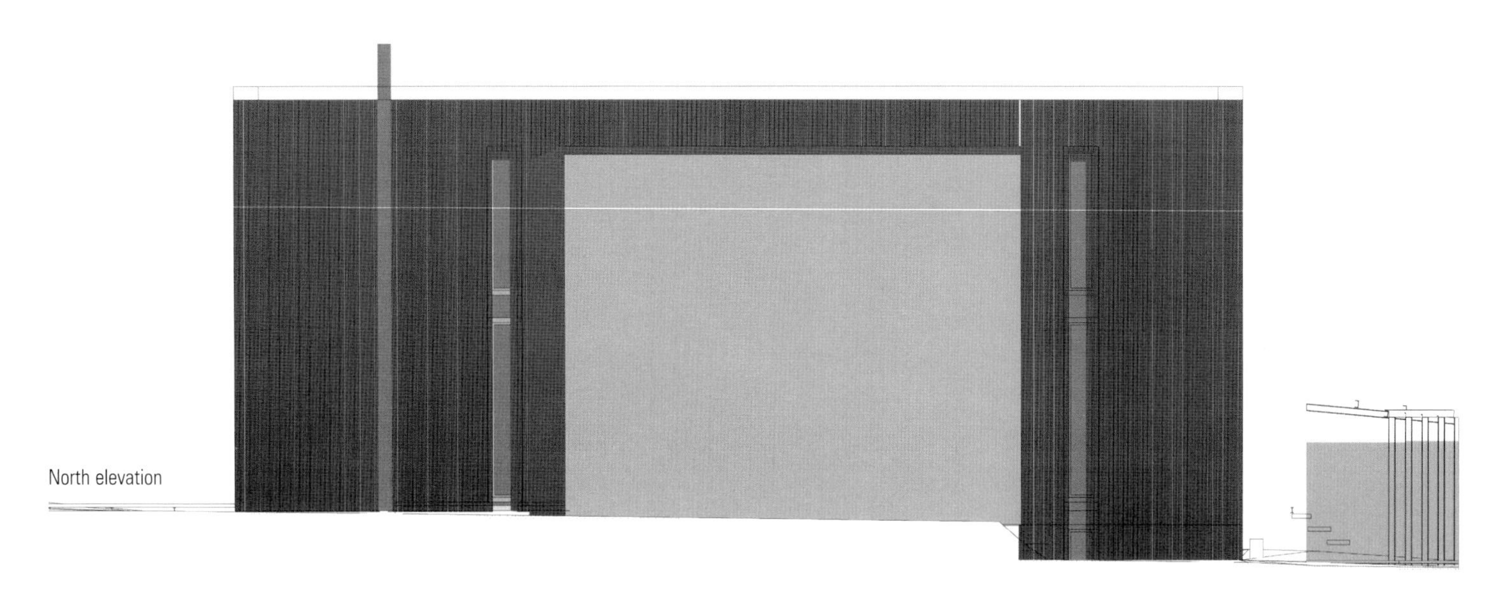

North elevation

Large, floor to ceiling windows allow maximum light into the living areas, and provide views to the nearby mountain. The distinctive red timber cladding and strong geometric shape distinguish the house from its pitched-roof neighbors.

East elevation

West elevation

South elevation

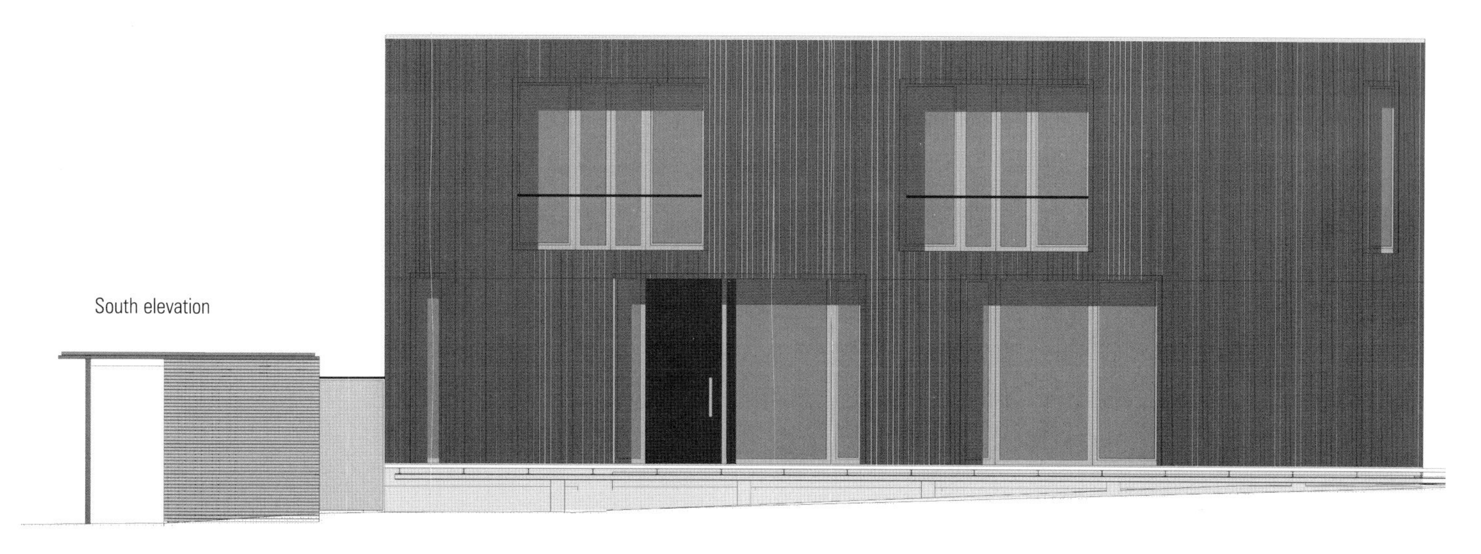

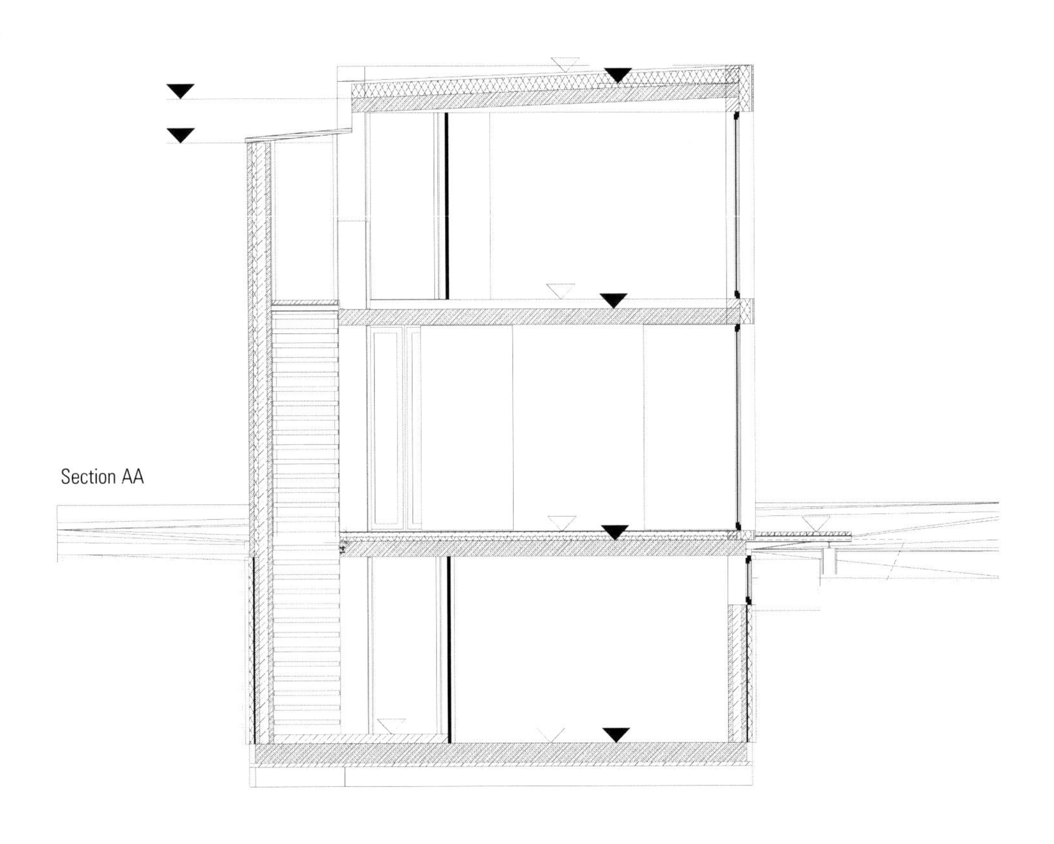
Section AA

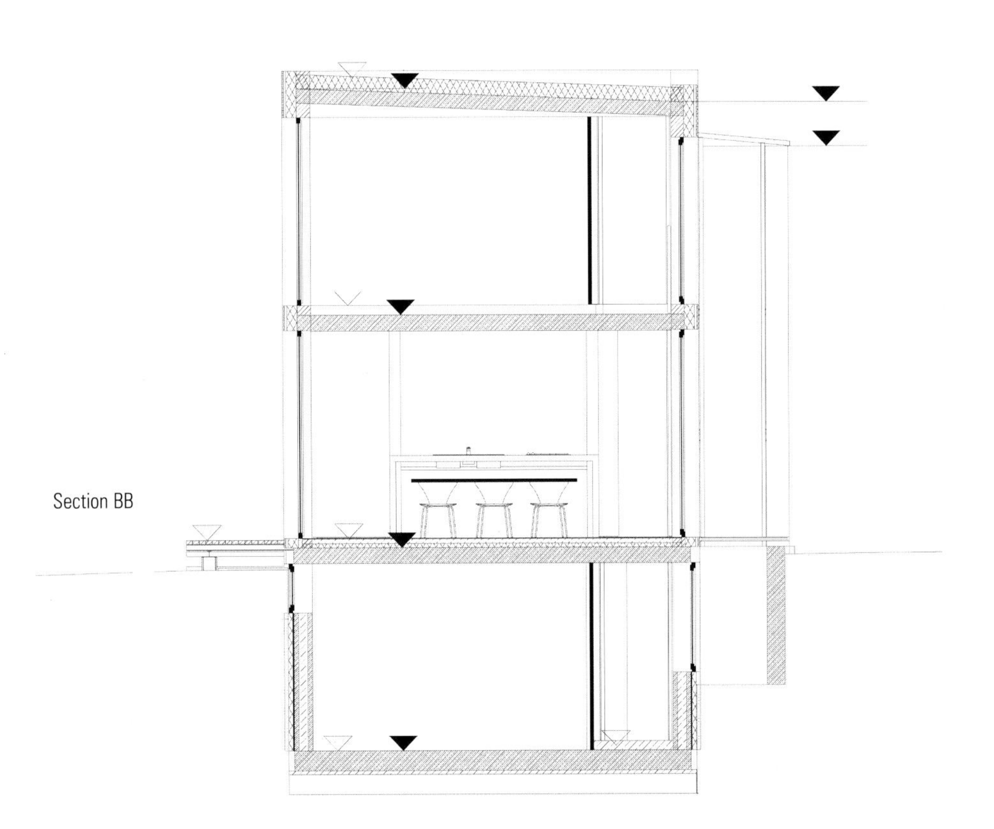
Section BB

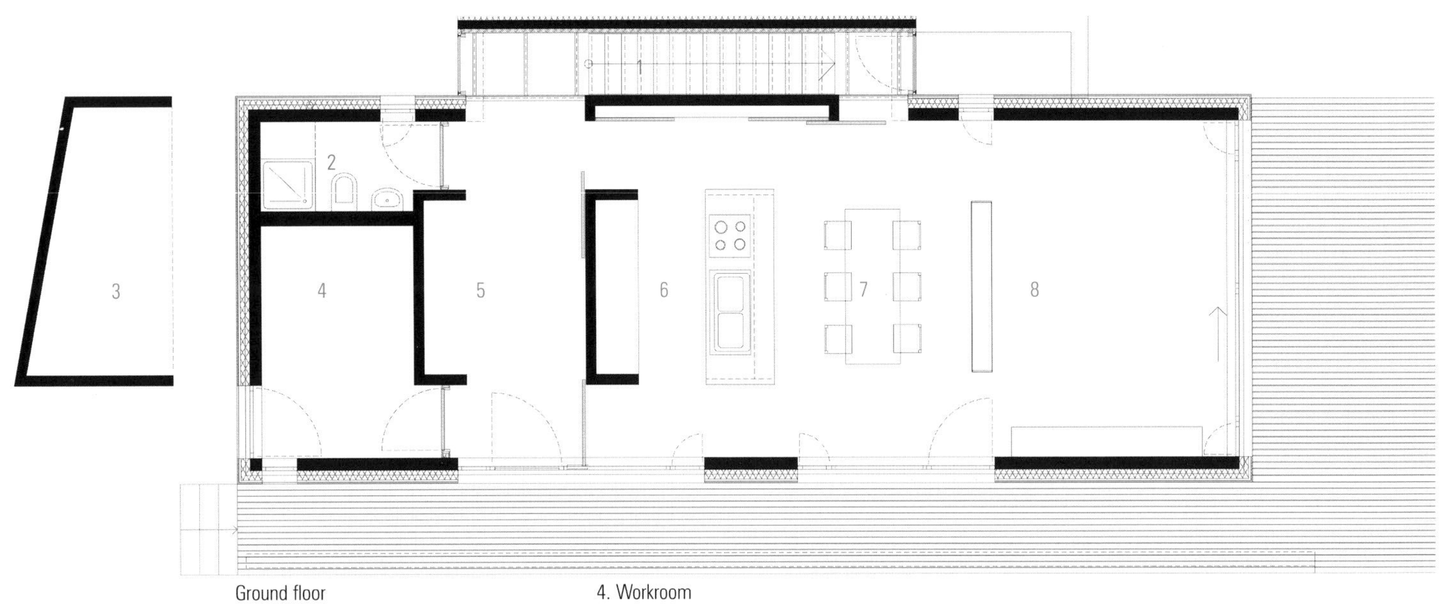

Ground floor
1. Stairway: 16 risers 0.184 m
15 treads 0.242 m
2. W C
3. Storage space
4. Workroom
5. Hall
6. Kitchen
7. Dining room
8. Living room

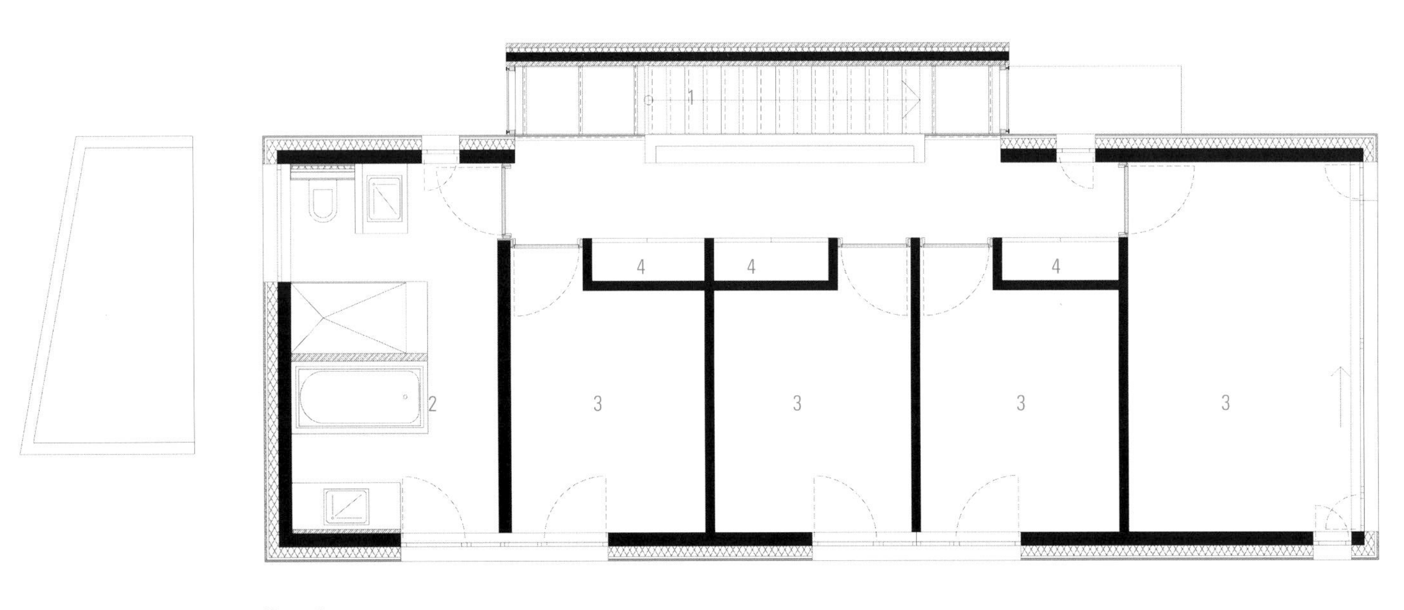

Upper floor
1. Stairway: 16 risers 0.184 m
15 treads 0.242 m
2. Bathroom
3. Bedrooms
4. Cupboards

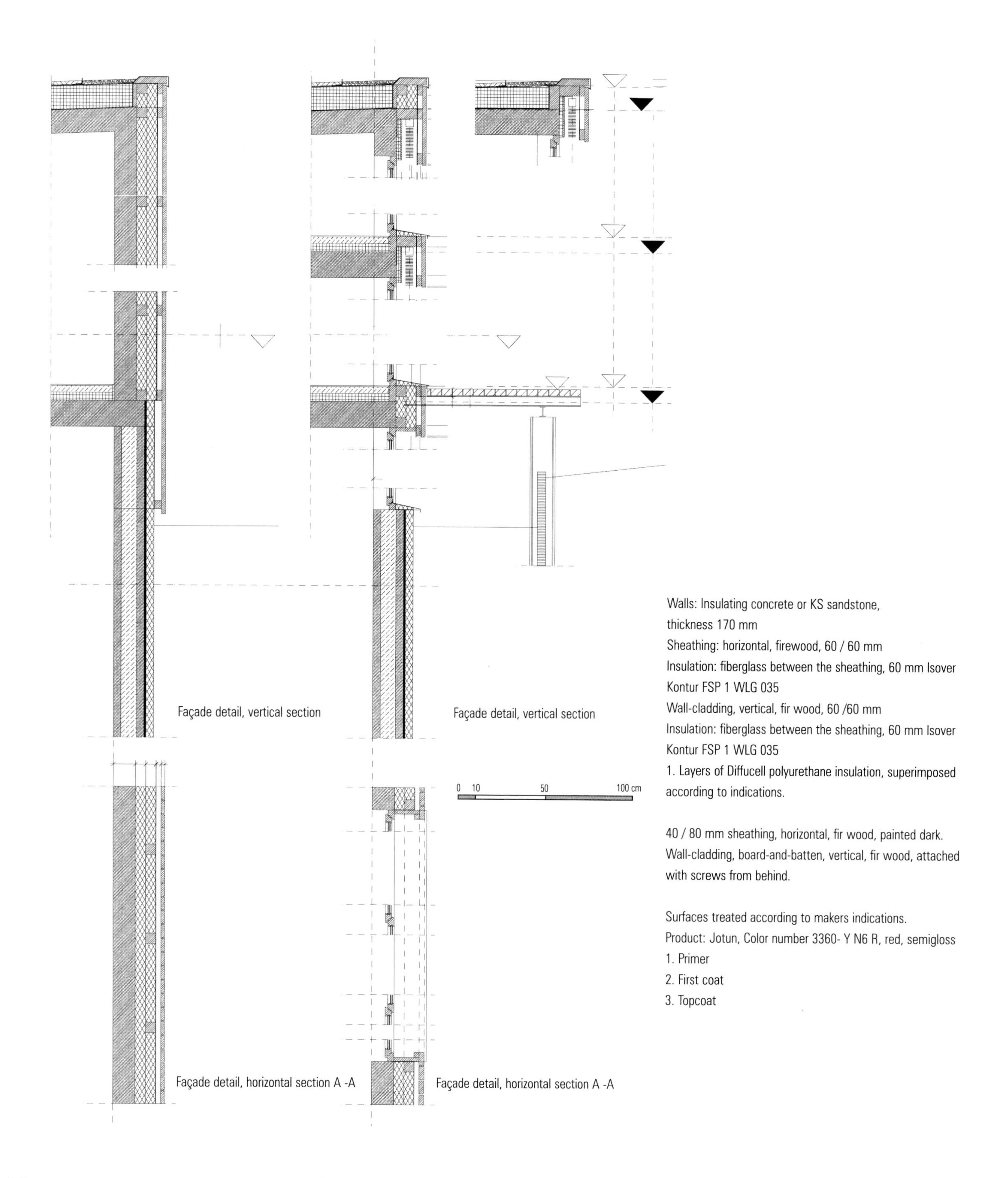

Façade detail, vertical section

Façade detail, vertical section

Façade detail, horizontal section A -A

Façade detail, horizontal section A -A

Walls: Insulating concrete or KS sandstone, thickness 170 mm
Sheathing: horizontal, firewood, 60 / 60 mm
Insulation: fiberglass between the sheathing, 60 mm Isover Kontur FSP 1 WLG 035
Wall-cladding, vertical, fir wood, 60 /60 mm
Insulation: fiberglass between the sheathing, 60 mm Isover Kontur FSP 1 WLG 035
1. Layers of Diffucell polyurethane insulation, superimposed according to indications.

40 / 80 mm sheathing, horizontal, fir wood, painted dark.
Wall-cladding, board-and-batten, vertical, fir wood, attached with screws from behind.

Surfaces treated according to makers indications.
Product: Jotun, Color number 3360- Y N6 R, red, semigloss
1. Primer
2. First coat
3. Topcoat

José Luis Canosa, Silvia Barbera

Housing in Begur

Begur, Spain

These four single-family houses try to resolve their functional program through an interpretation of the site and its topographical features. The way that the group of buildings adapts to the unevenness of the terrain makes it possible to read each unit, and its placement in relation to the others, as a juxtaposition of naturally occurring elements on the site.

The entrance to the group of buildings is through a landscaped area at street or ground level. The individual entrance to each house is at the intermediate level, through an area consisting of entrance hall, living-dining room, kitchen and bathroom. In each house, an upper floor contains three bedrooms and two bathrooms, and on the lower floor a bedroom-bathroom and storage room which leads directly out into the garden.

The way the buildings have been arranged in relation to each other makes the best use of the uneven site, while allowing the desired autonomy for each individual house.

Photographs: Jordi Canosa

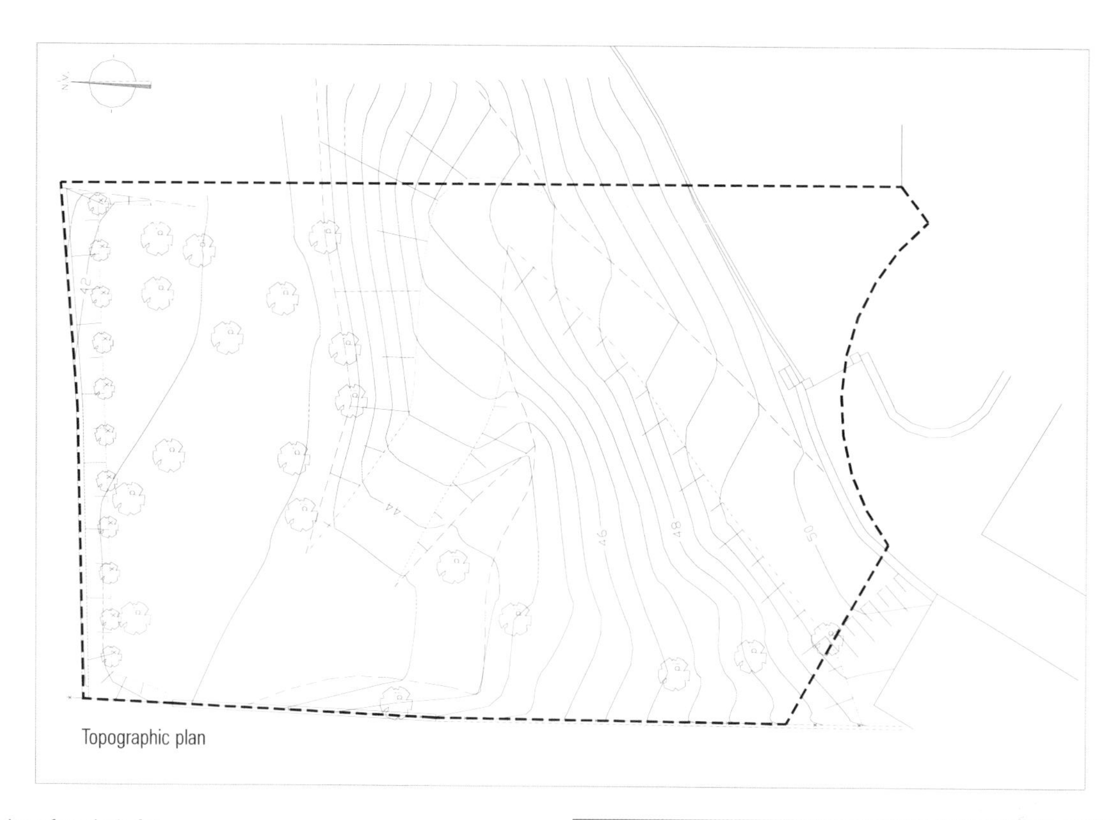

Topographic plan

The construction of these four single-family houses tries to resolve their functional program through the interpretation of the site and its topography.

Roof plan

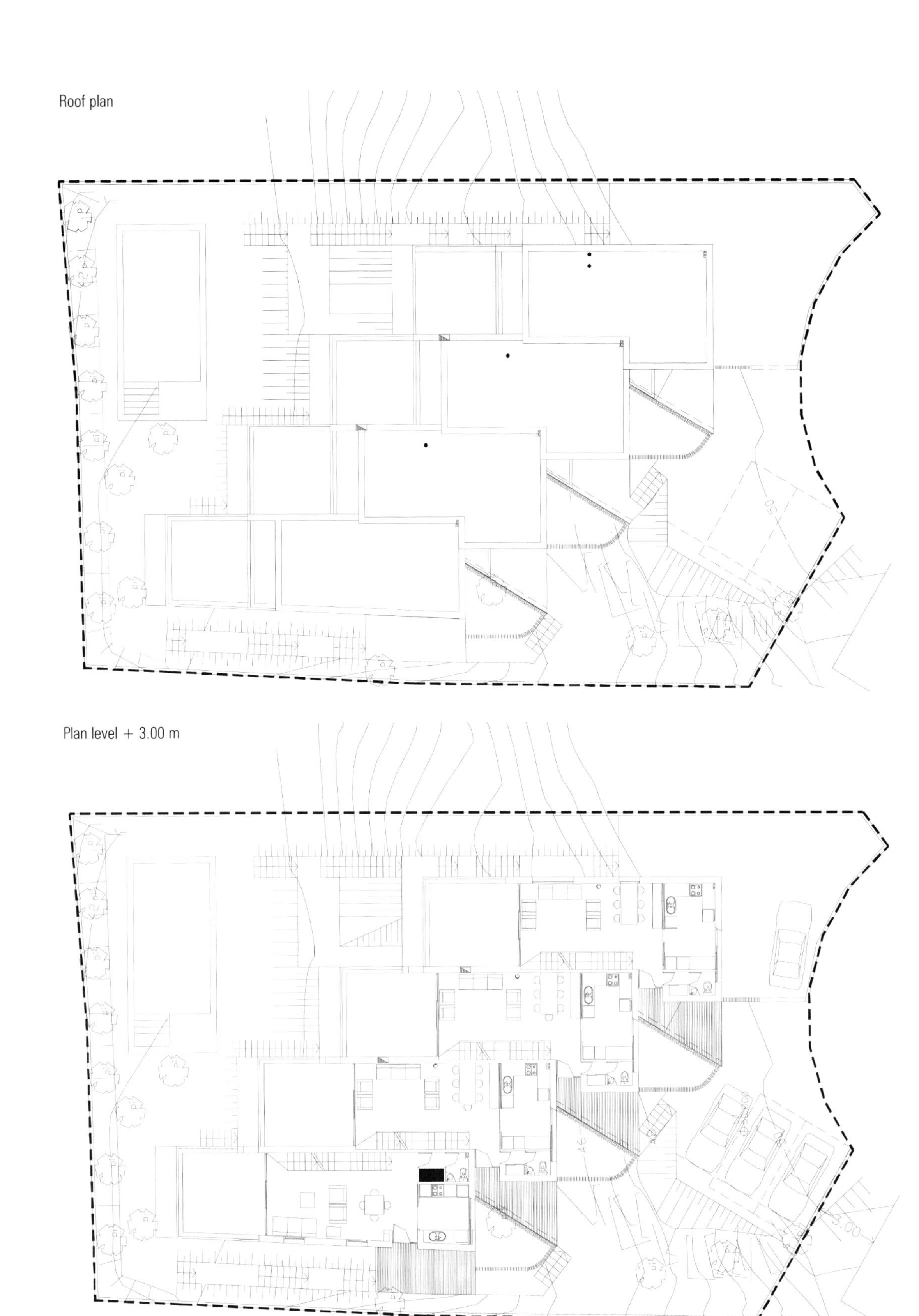

Plan level + 3.00 m

Plan level entry

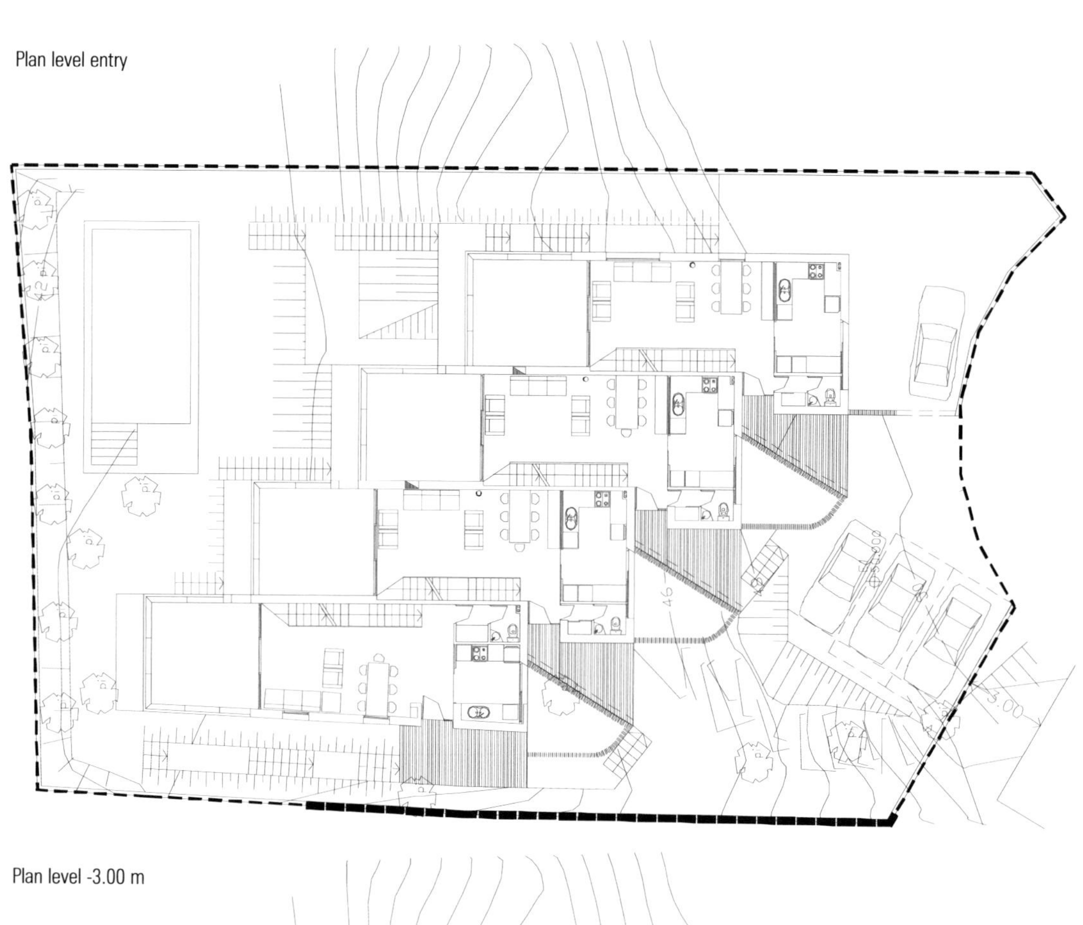

Plan level -3.00 m

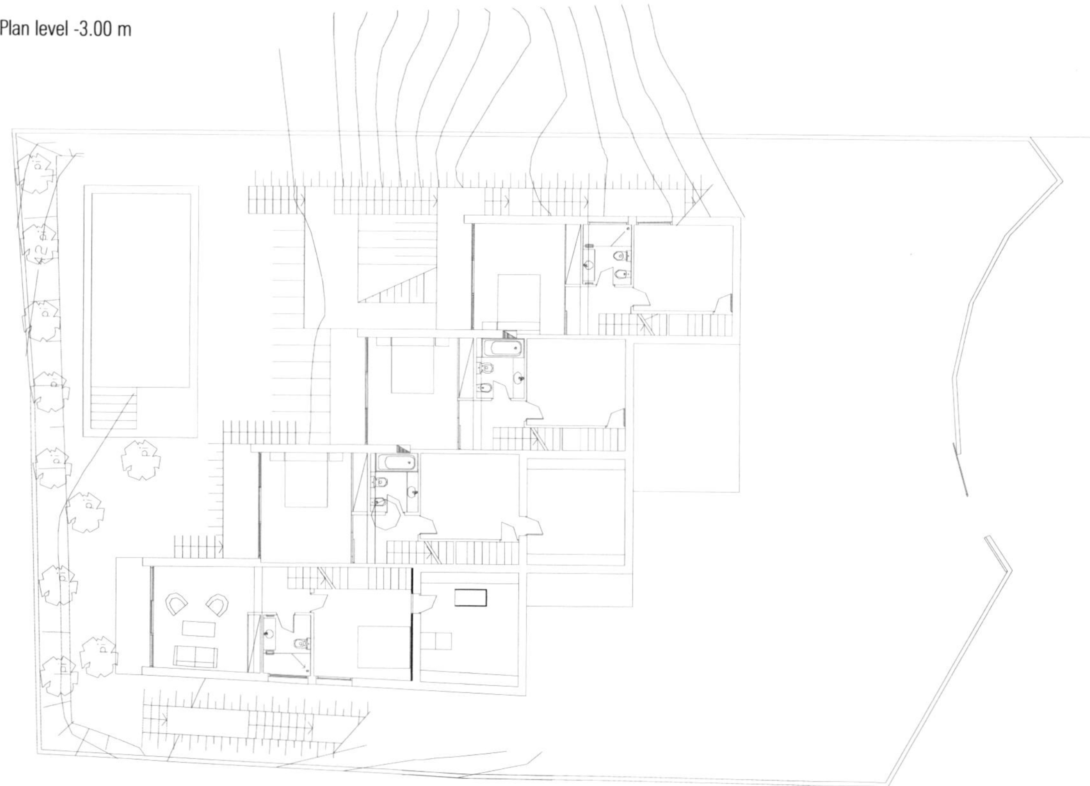

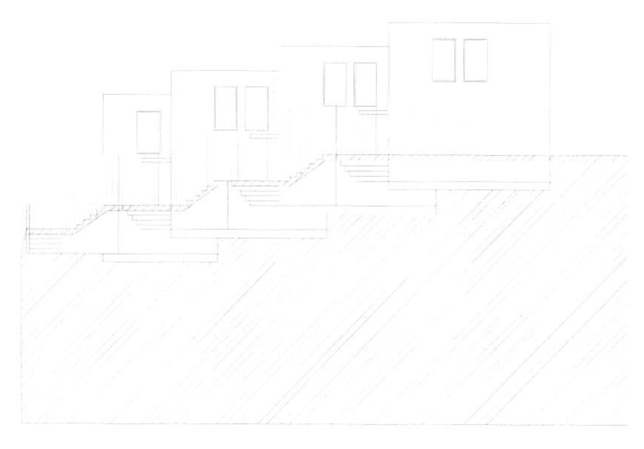

South elevation

West elevation

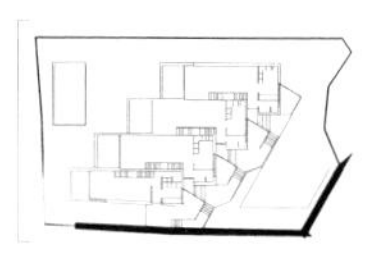

North elevation

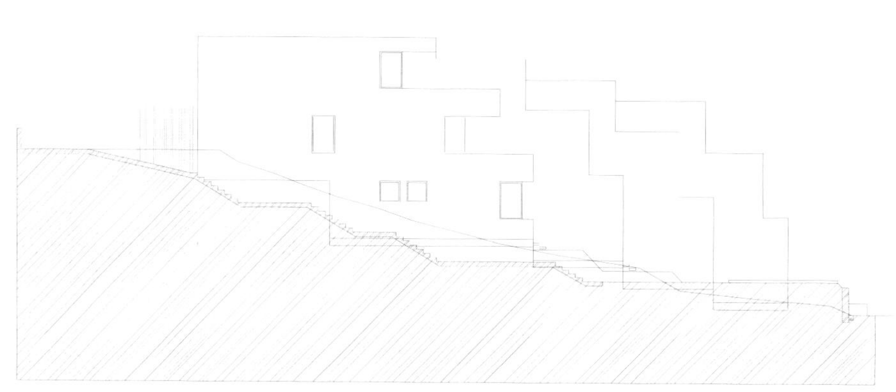

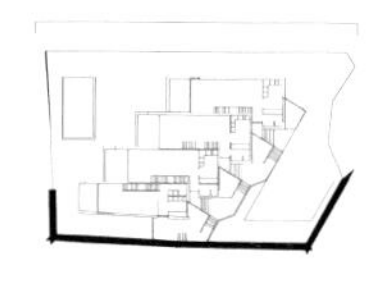

East elevation

The way each unit is composed and its placement relative to the others can be read as a juxtaposition of naturally occurring elements on the site.

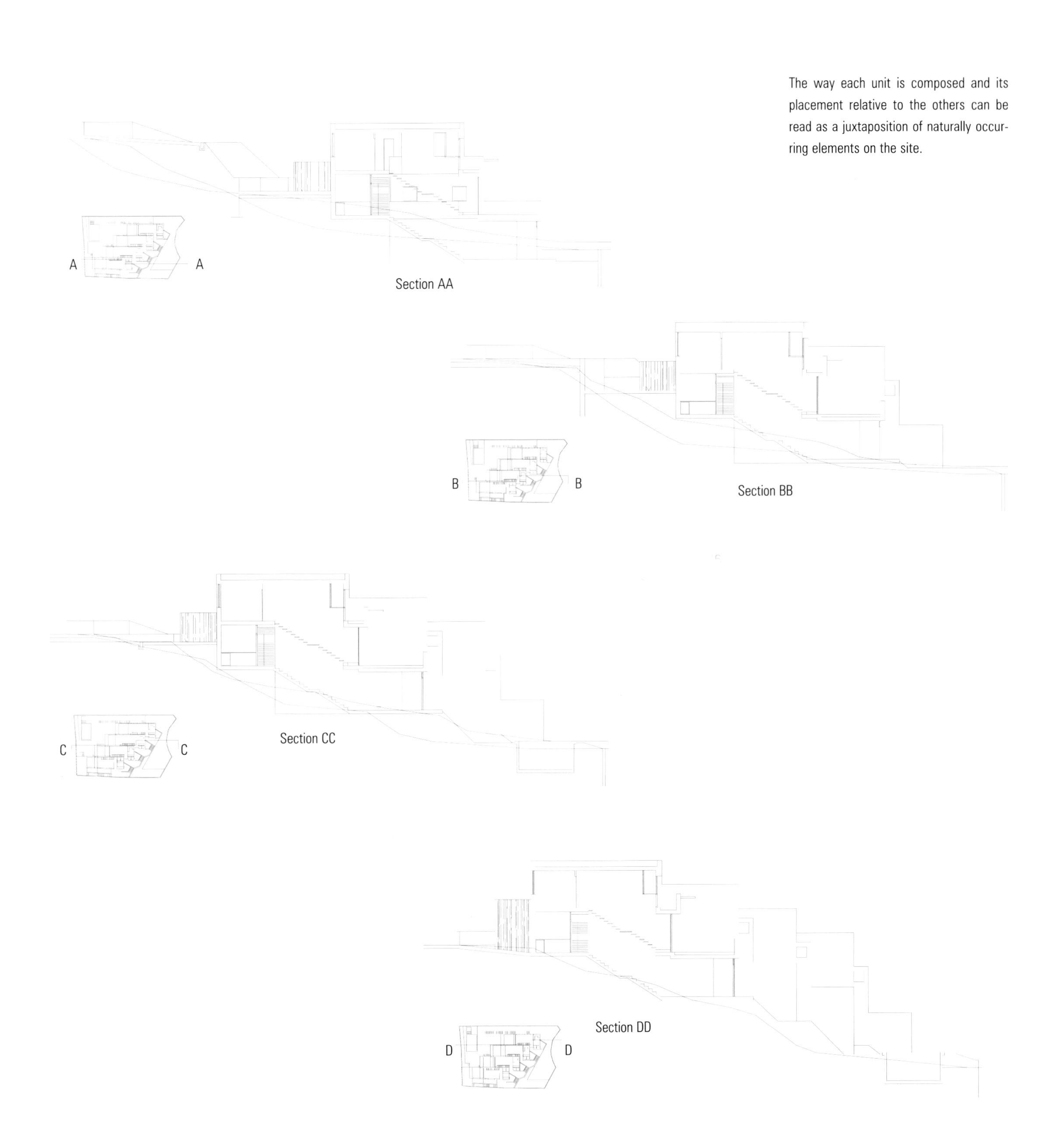

Chiba Manabu Architects

House in Black

Tokyo, Japan

This is a small house for a young couple on the outskirts of Tokyo, standing on a corner of a block at the end of a downhill road close to the Tama River. It is a simple cubic volume which involves three floor plates set on the center of the site.

The first floor has been scooped out as if to make a crossing integrated with the T-junction in front of the house. On the second floor, the skin has been peeled off to create windows and to bring the surrounding landscape into a more intimate relationship with the house.

There is also a slit cut out as a terrace on the third floor to mediate the two environmental elements that determine the character of this area; the hill and the river. Additionally, there are well holes at the four corners on the third floor, thereby making this level a bit smaller than the other two. Along with the staircase going through the center, a void connects the three floors gently and ambiguously.

The whole architecture composed in this way has an unstable outline and a permeable interior space. The architecture aims to create a new urban landscape that results from making a mutual relationship between the surrounding environment and itself. Furthermore, the idea was to merge the relationship between urban space and architecture, ensuring enclosed spaces for privacy while also creating a sense of transparency and views toward the public surroundings. This feeling of being both here and there, inside and out is one of the most essential charms of living in the city.

Photographs: Nacása & Partners

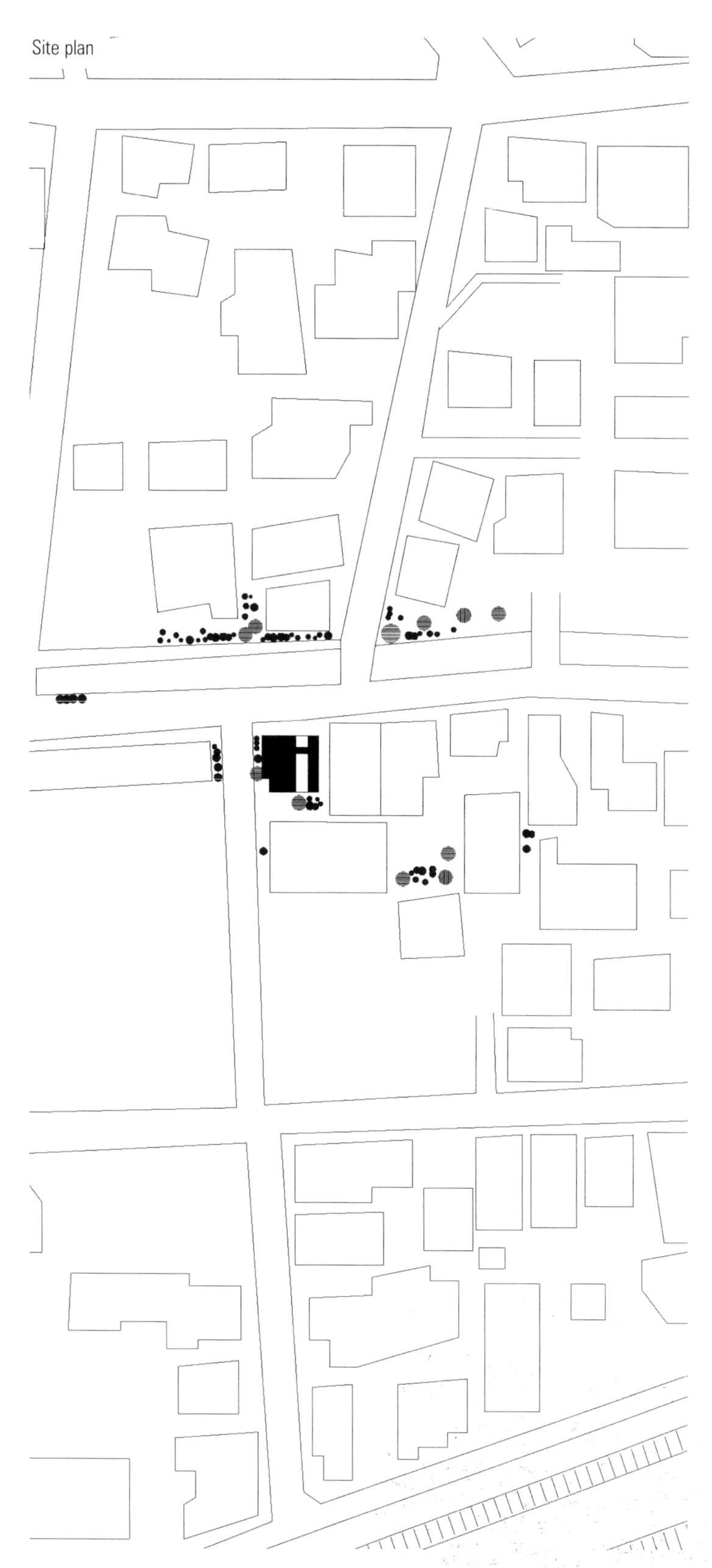
Site plan

Ground floor plan
1. Entrance
2. Porch
3. Corridor
4. Piano room
5. Studio
6. Toilet

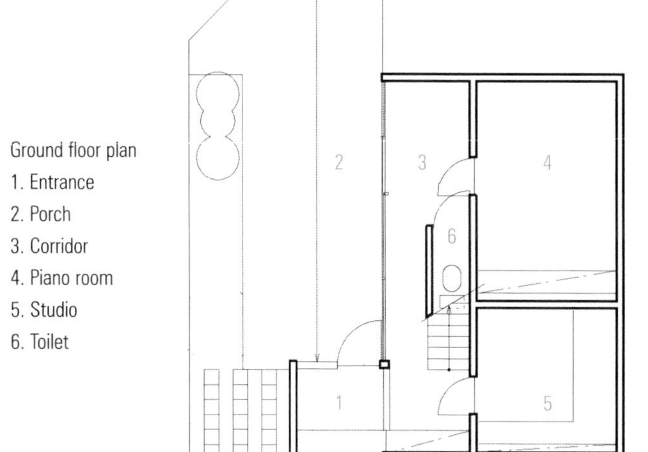

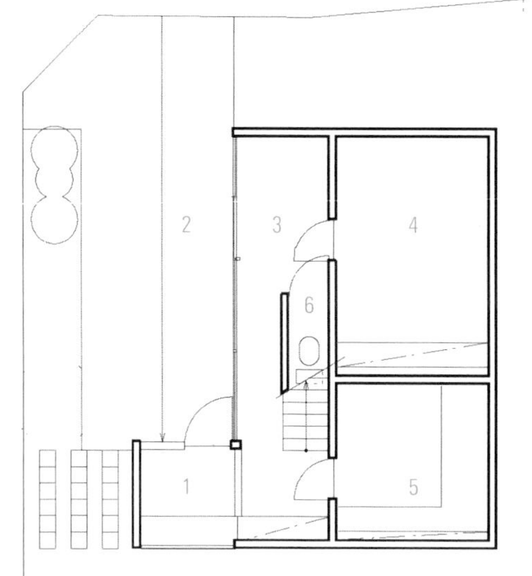

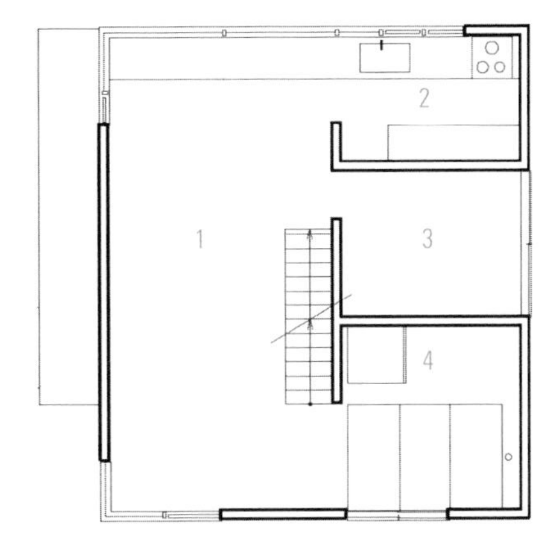

First floor plan
1. Living / Dining room
2. Kitchen
3. Child's room
4. Japanese style room

Second floor plan

1. Bed room
2. Void
3. Terrace
4. Corridor
5. Lavatory
6. Bathroom

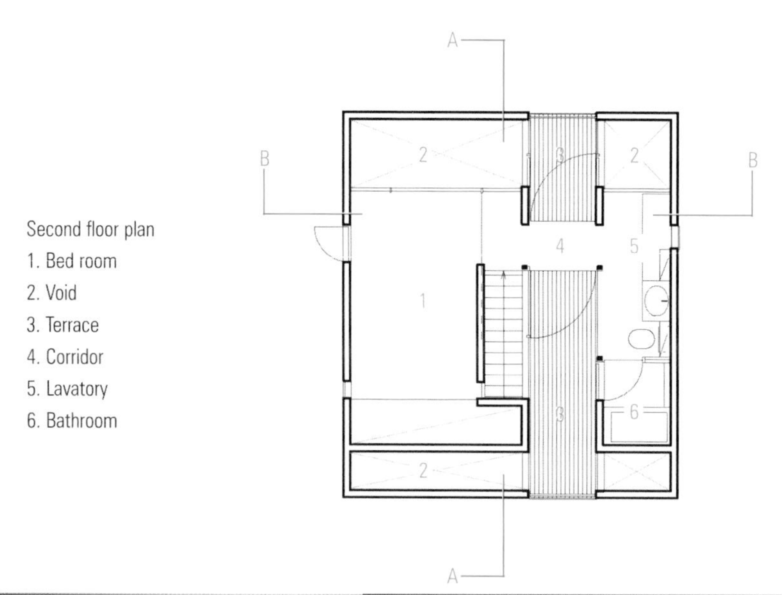

The house is based on a simple cubic volume that has been treated architecturally in order to respond to its environment. The metaphors of scooping out parts of the volume or peeling away the skin were applied to the basic shape in order to create an equilibrium between interior and exterior, house and surroundings.

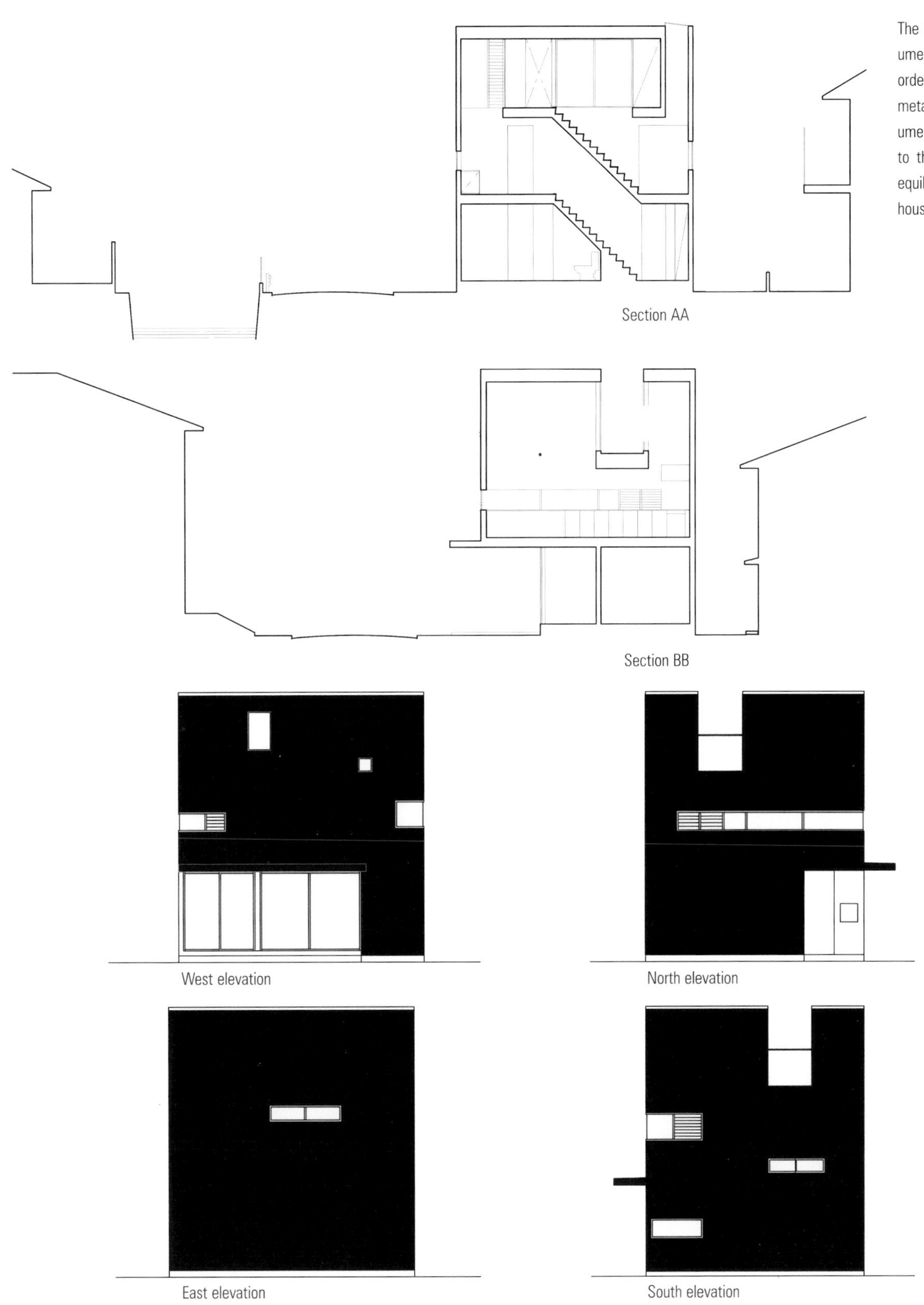

Olson Sundberg Kundig Allen Architects

Chicken Point Cabin

Northern Idaho, USA

The idea for the cabin is that of a lakeside shelter in the woods- a little box with a big window that opens to the surrounding landscape. The cabin's big window-wall (30 feet by 20 feet) opens the entire living space out toward the forest and lake. Materials are low maintenance (concrete block, steel, concrete floors and plywood) in keeping with the notion of a cabin, and left unfinished to naturally age and acquire a patina that fits in with the natural setting. The cabin sleeps ten.

Photographs: Benjamin Benschneider

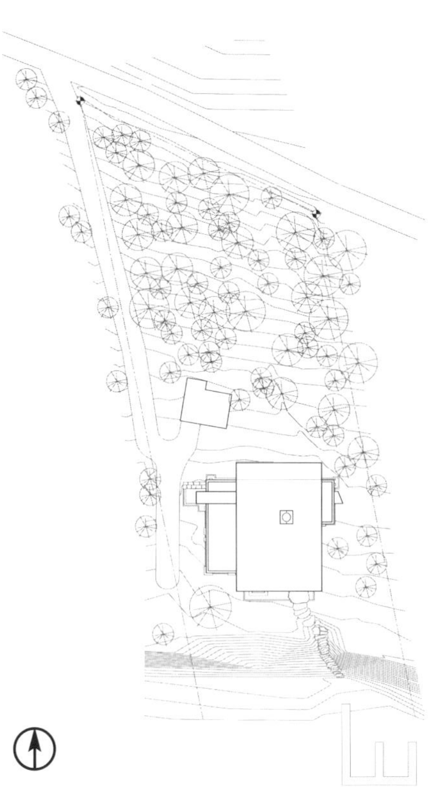

The guesthouse is located on the shore of a lake, surrounded by forest. The design's references to a log cabin, together with the large 6 x 9 meter windows opening out to the landscape, allow the buiding to interact with its surroundings and reinforce its relationship with the landscape.

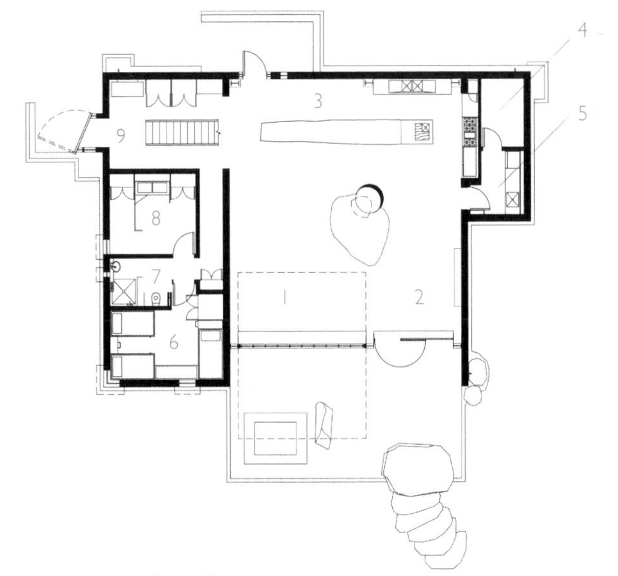

Ground floor plan

1. Living
2. Library/t.v.
3. Kitchen
4. Mechanical
5. Laundry/pantry
6. Bunk room
7. Bath
8. Guestroom
9. Entry

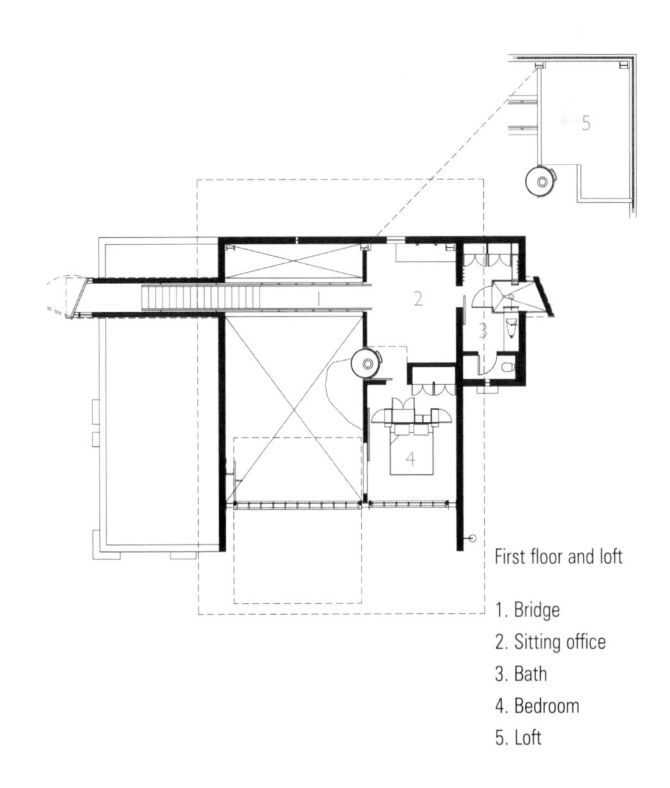

First floor and loft

1. Bridge
2. Sitting office
3. Bath
4. Bedroom
5. Loft

IRVING PENN

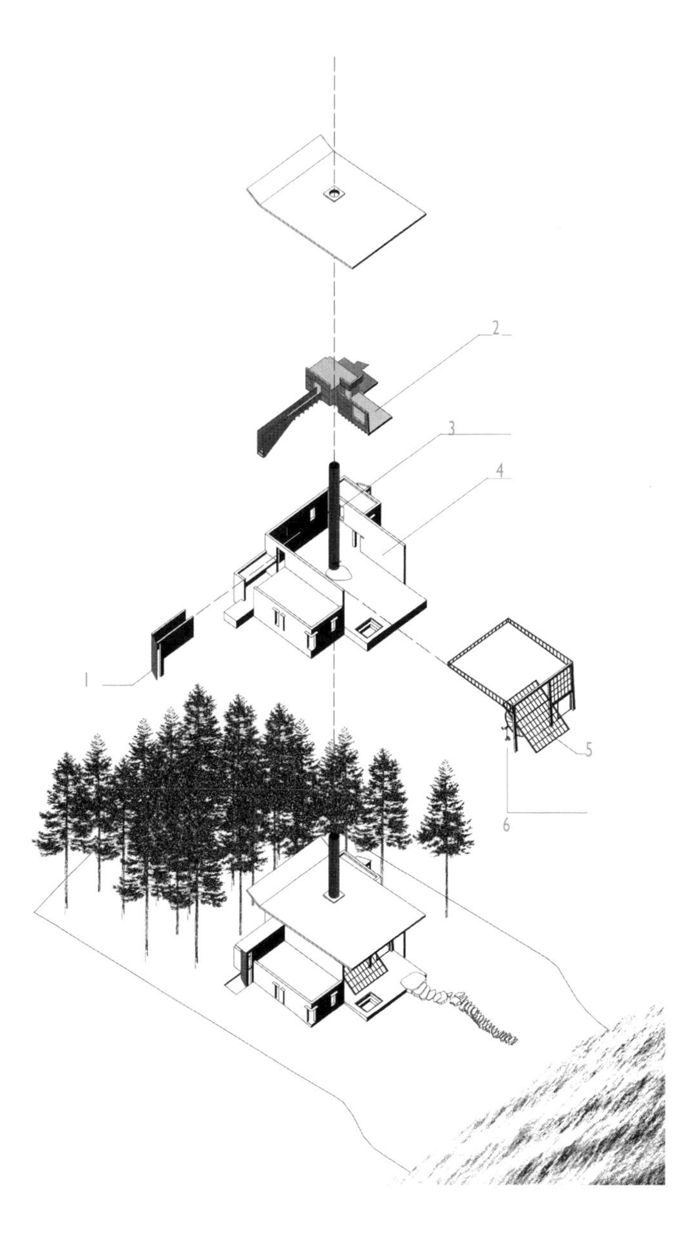

1. Big steel door
2. Wood loft
3. Steel bong
4. Concrete block
5. Big window
6. Gizmo

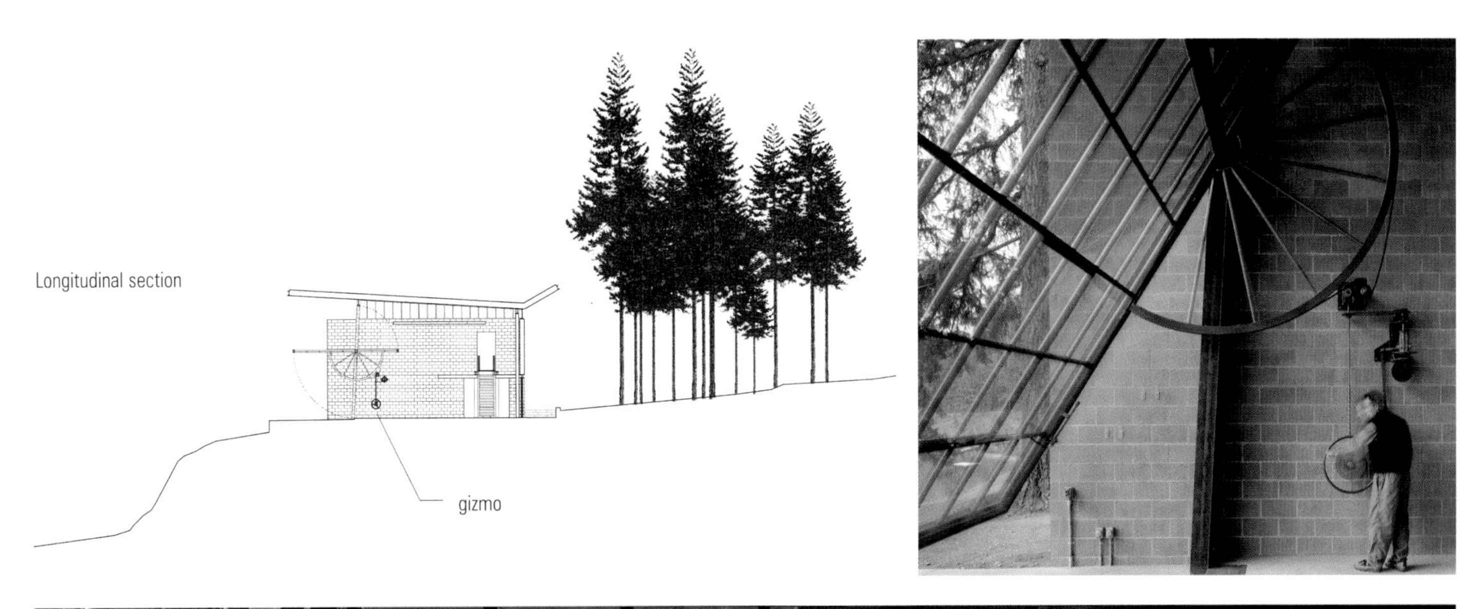
Longitudinal section
gizmo

Archi-Tectonics

Gypsy Trail Guesthouse

Kent, USA

This guesthouse is located on a site in Croton Reservoir, upstate New York, where hills tumble straight into the lake in a lakefront landscape that alternates green patches with craggy rock formations. The guesthouse is built as an 'alter-ego' of a larger structure; the main house, situated right on the lake. Conceived as similar in materials as the house it forms the easy-going, basic version of its more sophisticated 'other'.

The 1,500 square foot building is designed as a stone base volume (2-car garage), which supports a cantilevering cedar wood structure, backpack-like, the split level guesthouse. The light-weight guest house hovers over the ground and cantilevers off of the garage constructed of rough stone collected from the site.

This split-level volume of wood and glass hovers free with a small porch extending into the landscape. The void behind the double height glass wall connects the living room above to the sleeping area at the ground floor, where large sliding doors allow for direct access to the garden and the lake beyond. To take advantage of the spectacular views, the living area is lifted up to the second floor with the dining / kitchen area opening up to a terrace on top of the garage providing a generous seating area with a 'surround' view of the site.

The layered front façade of the guesthouse creates a filtered entrance area; a cantilevering asymmetrical cedar overhang protects from north winds. The double height large glass façade is set back and allows for sun rays to penetrate far into the intimate space, and felt curtains in the double height space create a soft supple boundary between interior and exterior spaces. The house is finished inside and out with cedar wood, allowed to slowly turn silver over time.

Photographs: Winka Dubbeldam

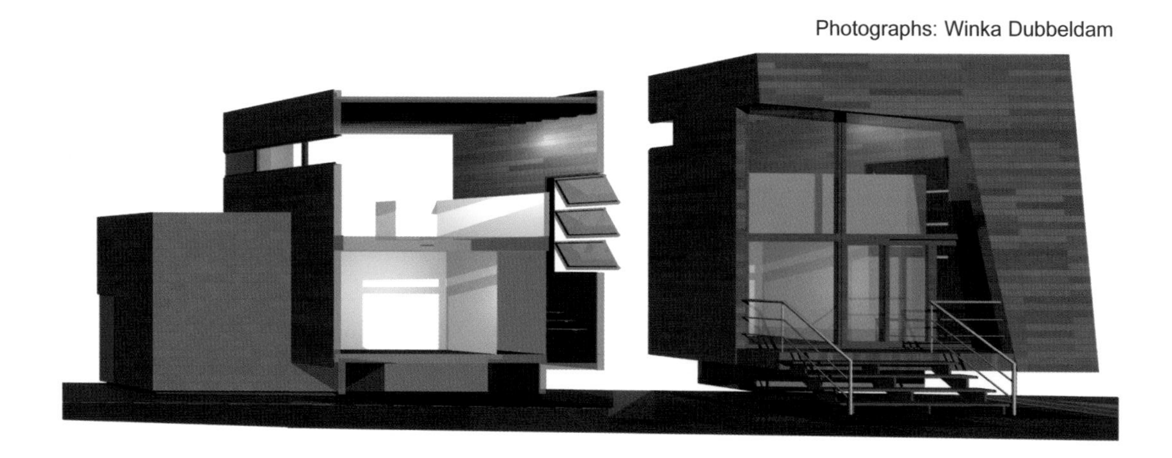

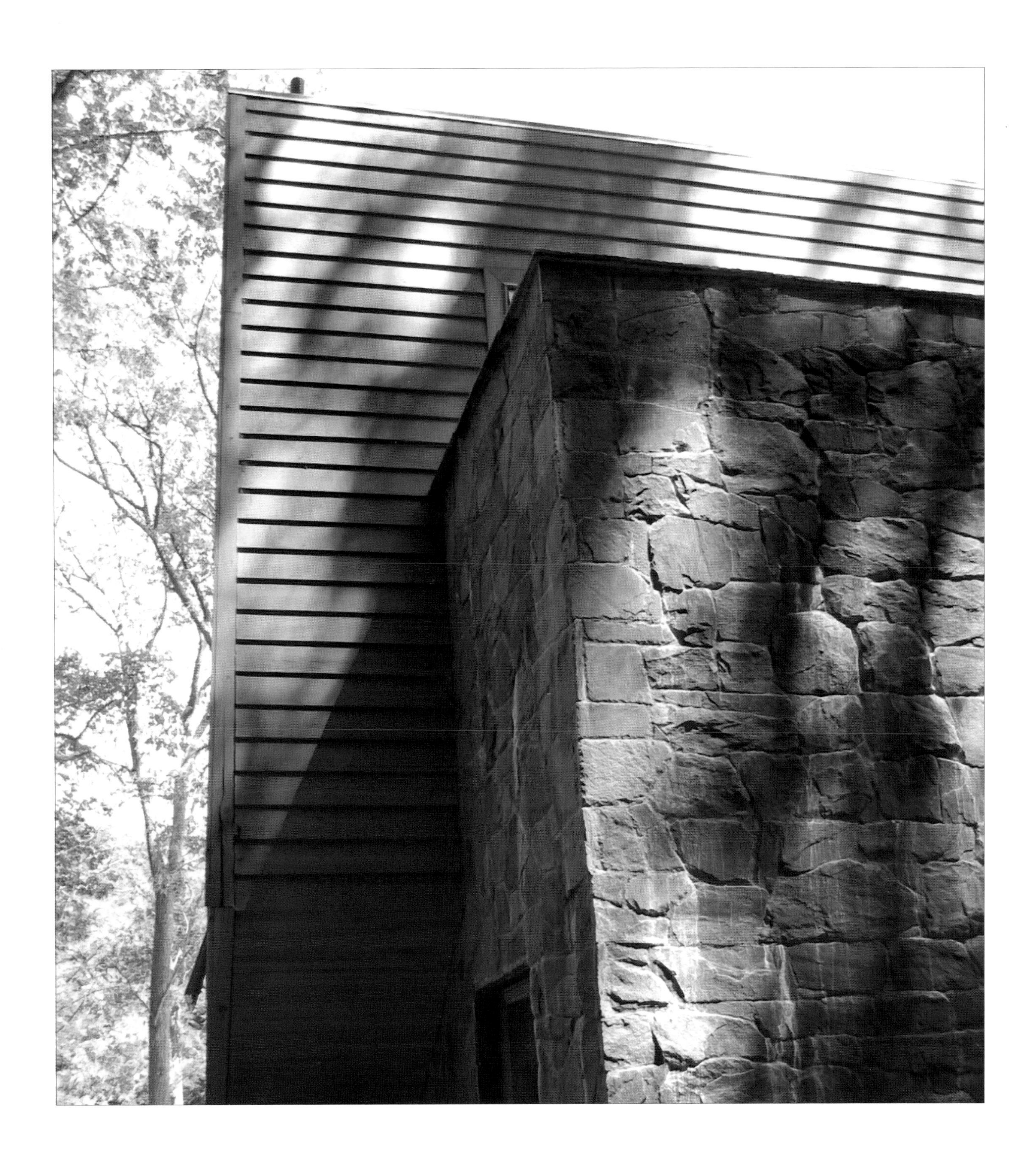

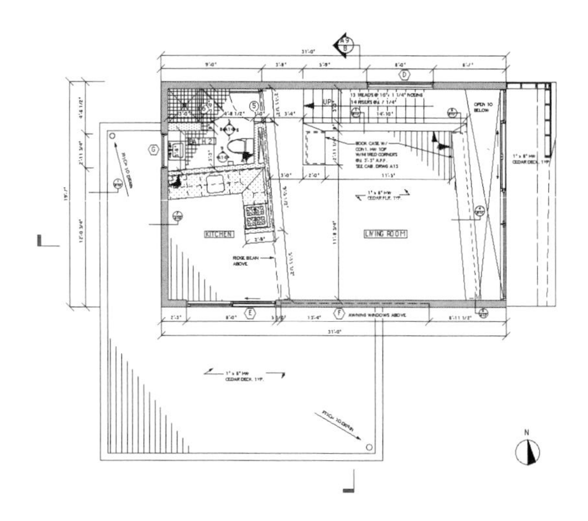

First floor plan

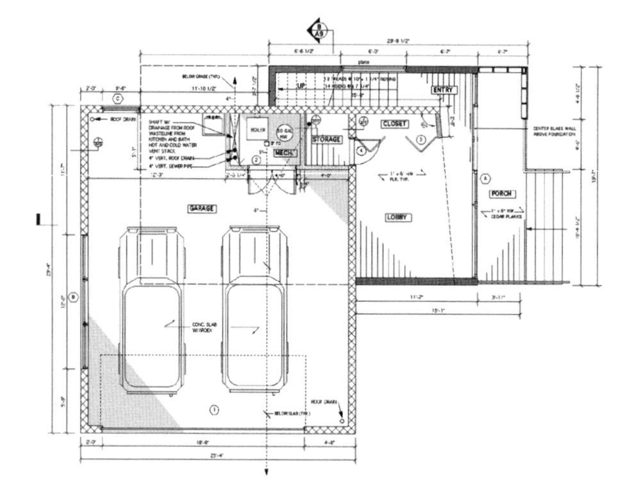

Ground floor plan

The light-weight cedar wood guesthouse hovers over the ground and cantilevers off of the garage, which is constructed using rough stone collected from the site. A glass façade and terrace take advantage of the spectacular surroundings.

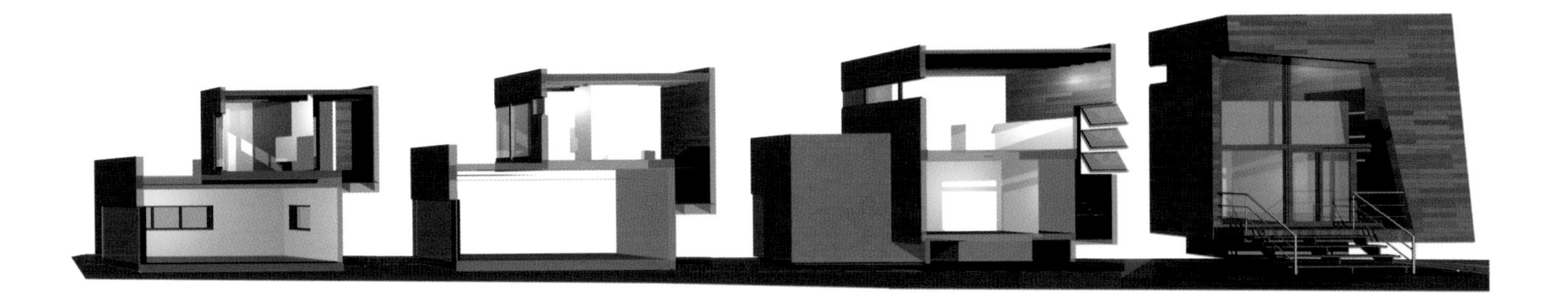

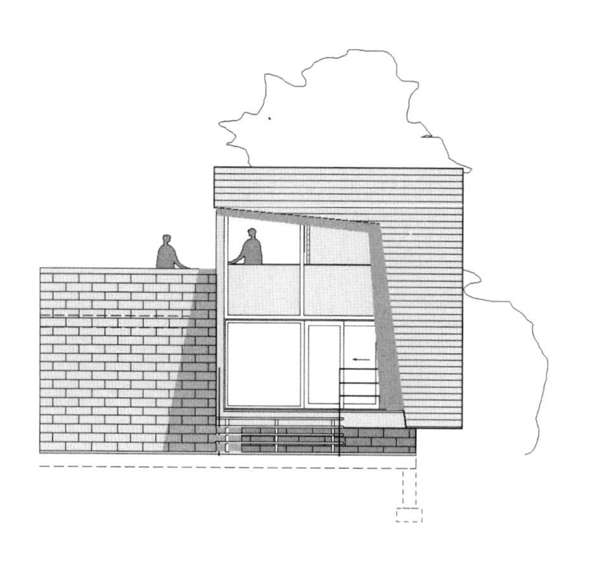

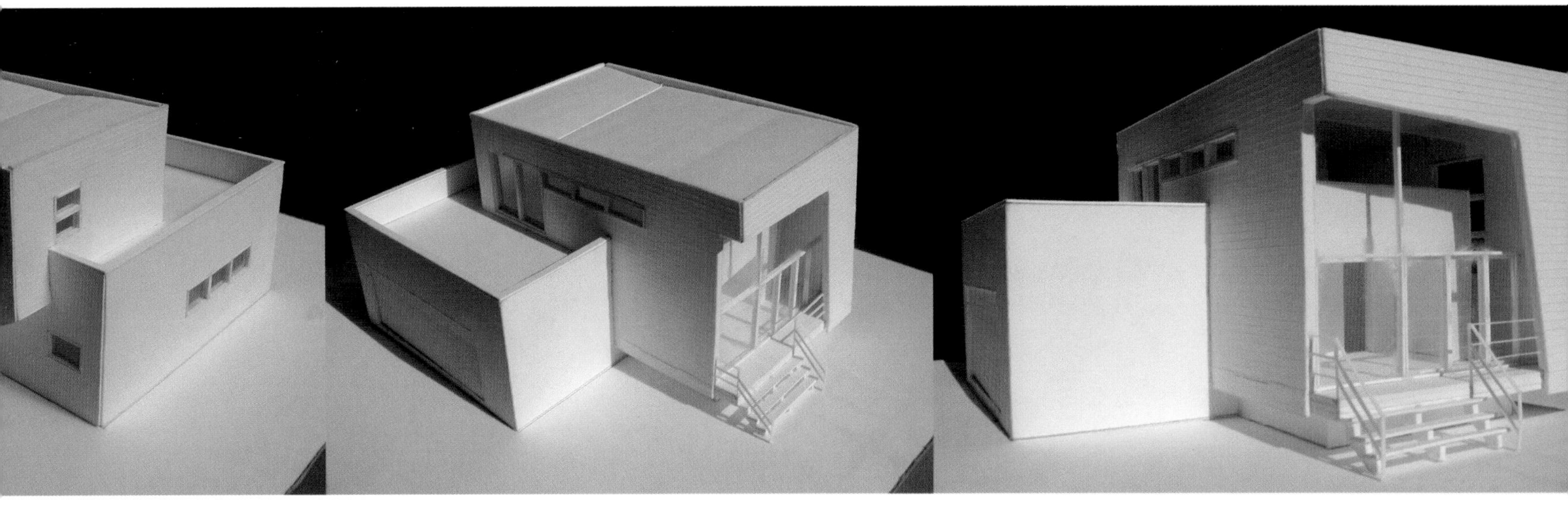

Featherstone Associates

Voss Street House

London, UK

A mixed use development on a site comprising a shop facing onto Bethnal Green Road, a self-contained studio and a two-bedroom house above. The architect (also the home's owner) had to address two primary concerns in the design: the need for privacy from the busy commercial street and overcoming the serious spatial limitations presented by a plot which was only 4 meters wide.

The site's spatial restrictions were resolved by the creation of high-ceilinged, diaphanous spaces, entirely free of connecting corridors. Instead, a lozenge-shaped spiral staircase was built -most of its volume jutting out into the central courtyard- providing access to each individual level.

Privacy, as well as abundant natural light, have been achieved by arranging the rooms around the central courtyard, with all windows facing inward. There are no windows in the south-facing elevation; while the only window on the north facade has been fitted with etched glass in order to filter light in while blocking views of the street outside. The house is a retreat which turns its back on the street, while also providing a generosity of light, space and materiality within the constraints of an awkward site.

Photographs: Tim Brotherton

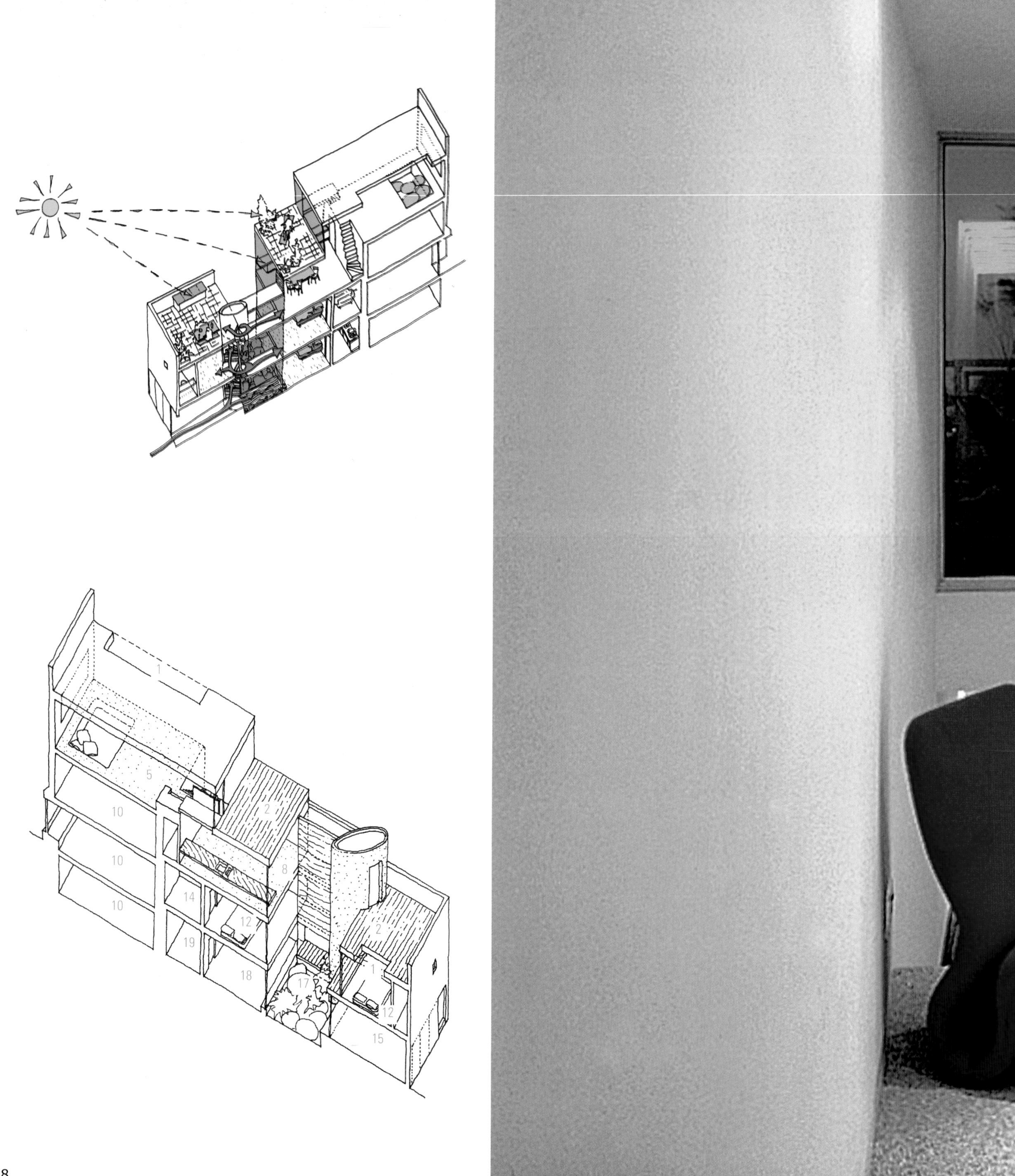

1
5
10
2
10
8
10
14
12
2
19
1
18
17
12
15

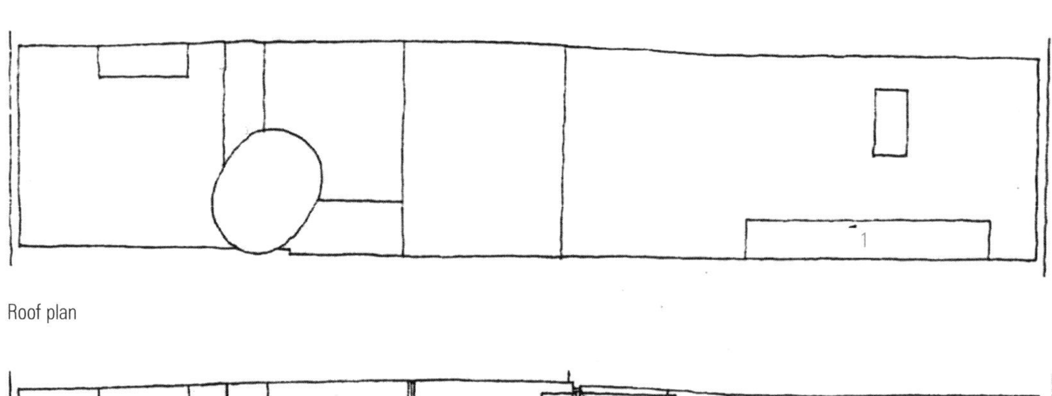

Roof plan

1. Rooflight
2. Roof terrace
3. Bridge
4. Double-height void
5. Living room
6. Conversation pit
7. Landing
8. Kitchen-dining
9. WC
10. Retail unit
11. Bathroom
12. Bedroom
13. Balcony
14. Dressing room
15. Garage-store
16. Entrance hall
17. Courtyard
18. Studio
19. Utility room

Second-third floor plan

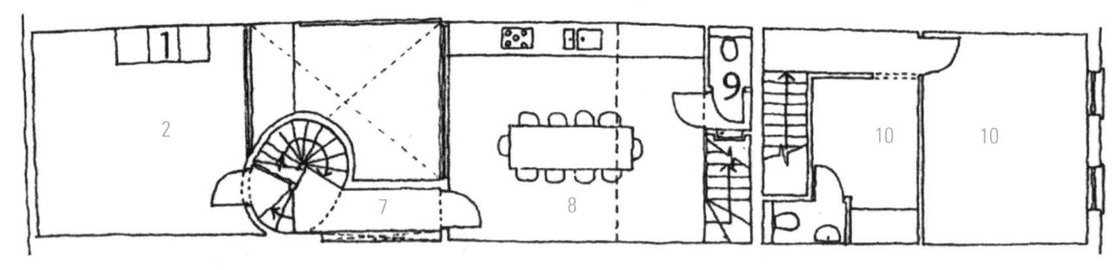

First-second floor plan

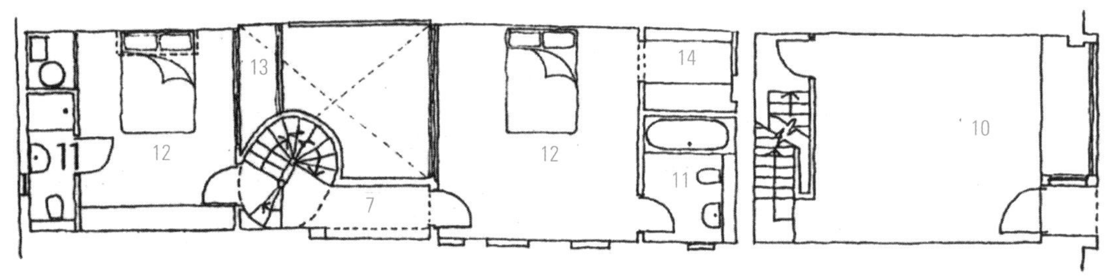

Upper ground-first floor plan

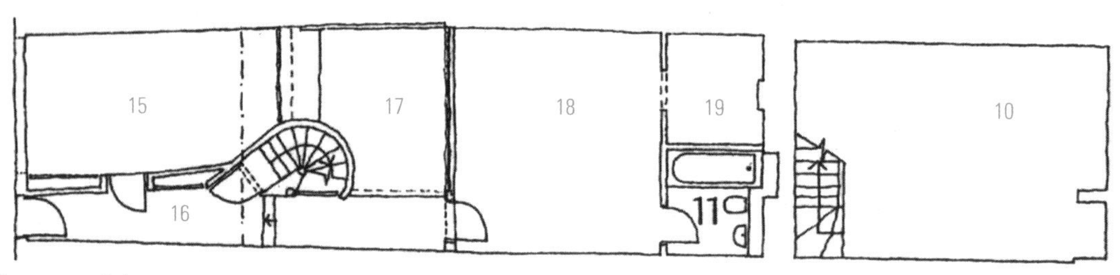

Lower ground plan

To ensure privacy and bring more light into the building, the rooms are arranged around a central courtyard, stacked one above the other at staggered half levels, all looking inwards.

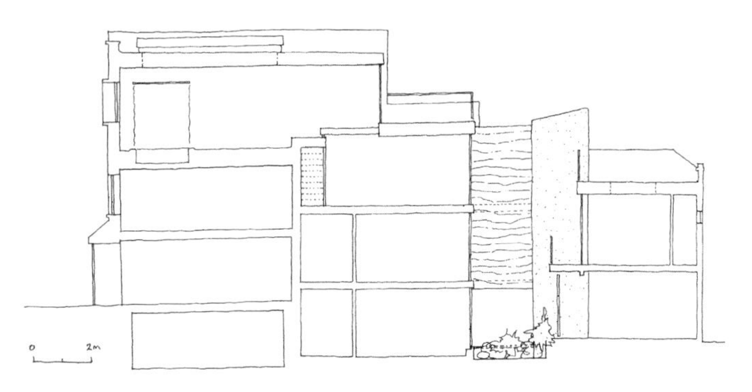

Longitudinal section

Because of the small scale, there was no room for corridors; thus, the first floor kitchen flows seamlessly into the second floor living room via an open staircase, with a toilet wedged into the nook at the top of the stairs. During the day, the kitchen thereby receives light from the picture window at the end of the house.

EM2N Architects

Holiday Cottage in the Swiss Alps

Flumserberg, Switzerland

This holiday house located next to an alpine pasture that serves as a ski slope in winter was specifically designed to address the surrounding landscape and topography. Unlike many standard holiday houses, it rises up high to catch the sun and the spectacular views on all sides. Around the house, the alpine pasture is left intact and the boundary of the site is not marked, so neighbors can ski across the site towards the ski slopes in winter. The house establishes a dialogue with the space, with the volume bending in order to welcome the swing of the hillside. The exterior develops the omnipresent style of low wide chalet house with dark wooden cladding and small windows into the image of a dark wooden tower with great openings.

The design also addresses the function of the house, creating spaces that adapt to holiday living. The garage is developed to be used as an outdoor-indoor play room in summer. The sleeping floor accommodates up to eight people in a large double-height space that also contains a bathroom, with the bathtub and spiral stair dividing the space into two areas.
On the living floor, which reads like a miniature house inside a house with its pitched roof, the kitchen and fireplace divide the space. There is a spatial progression from the dark, artificially lit garage to the sleeping floor with small windows on to the light-flooded living floor with views to the surrounding landscape.

Photographs: Hannes Henz

2303
2575
2500
2030
2039
2323
2279
3218
2769
2280
2322
2091
3463
2321
2158
2302
3347
3378
2320
2281

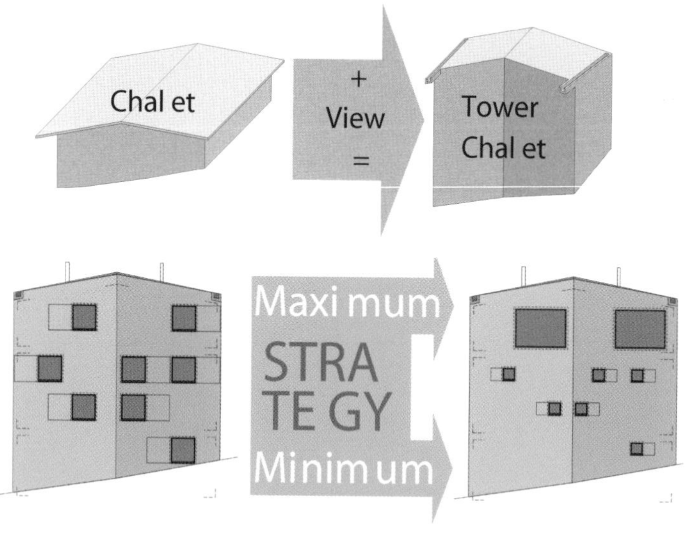
Chal et
+
View
=
Tower
Chal et
Maxi mum
STRA
TE GY
Minim um

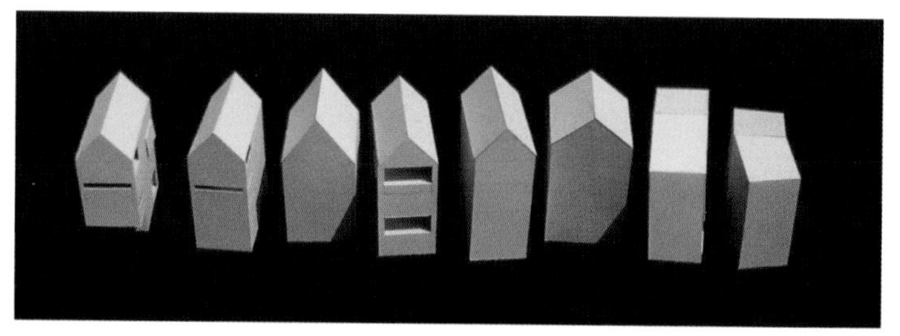

The floor plan is an irregular shape, bending slightly in response to the topography of the site. The layout allows flexibility in order to adapt to holiday living. A spiral staircase connects the basement and ground levels to the top living area, which has large windows that provide views to the surrounding landscape.

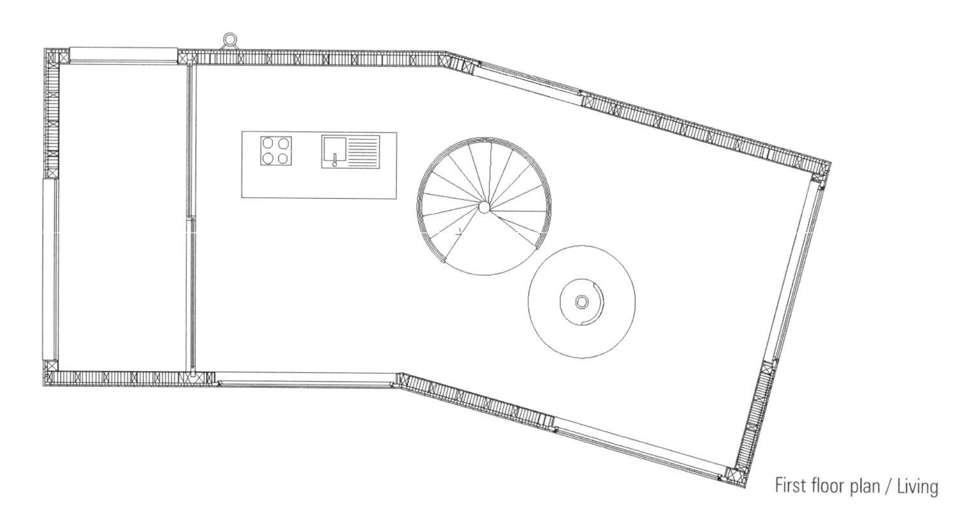

First floor plan / Living

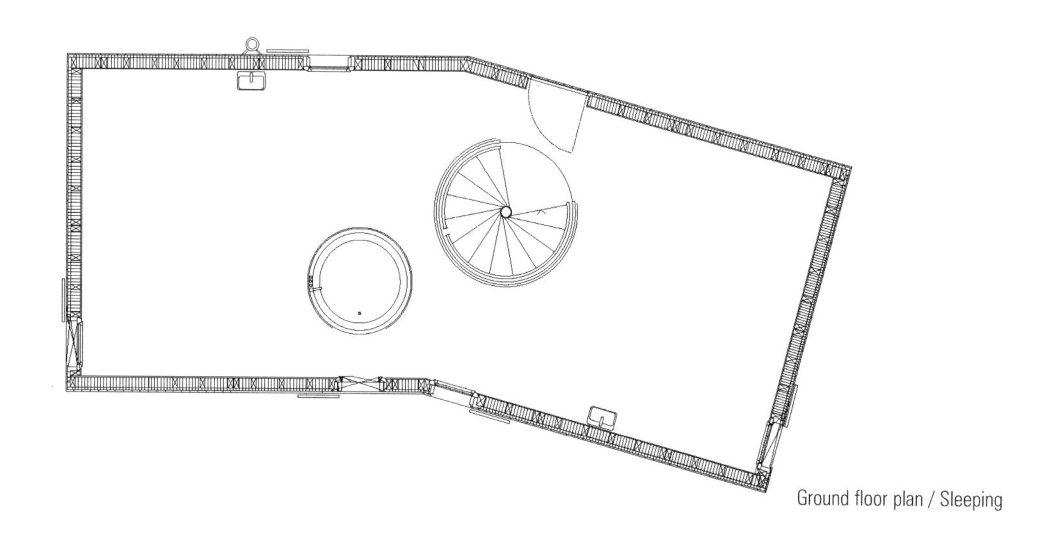

Ground floor plan / Sleeping

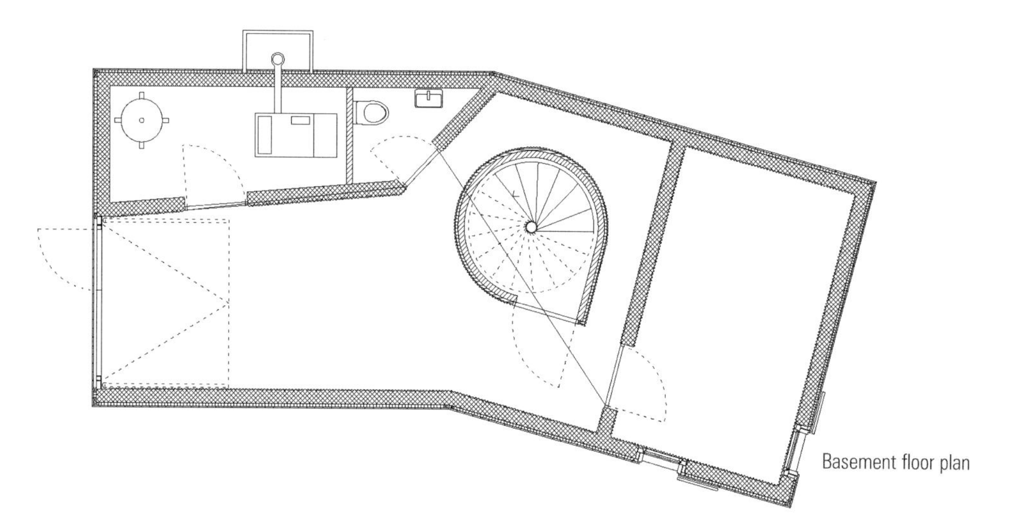

Basement floor plan

0 1 2 5 m

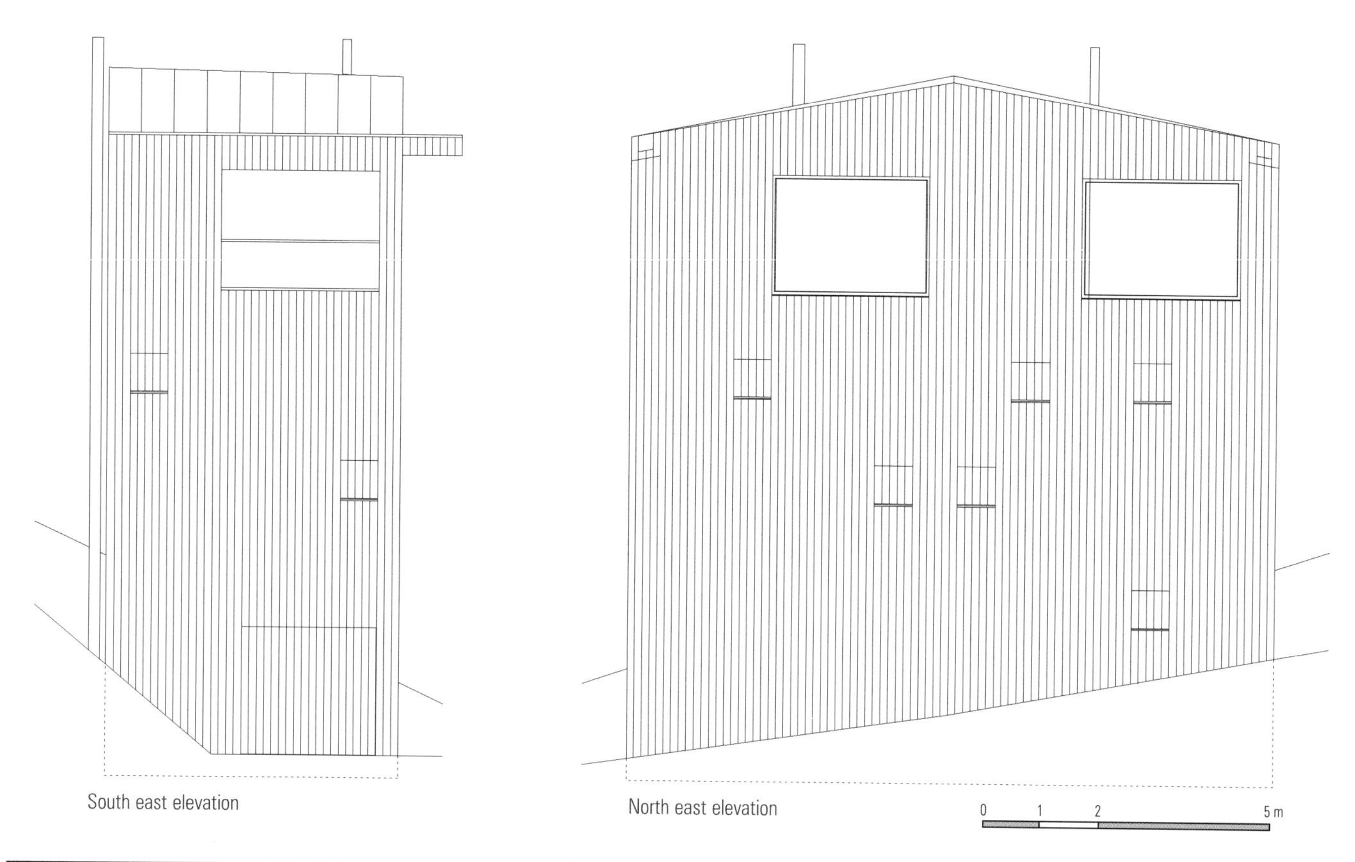
South east elevation
North east elevation
0
1
2
5 m

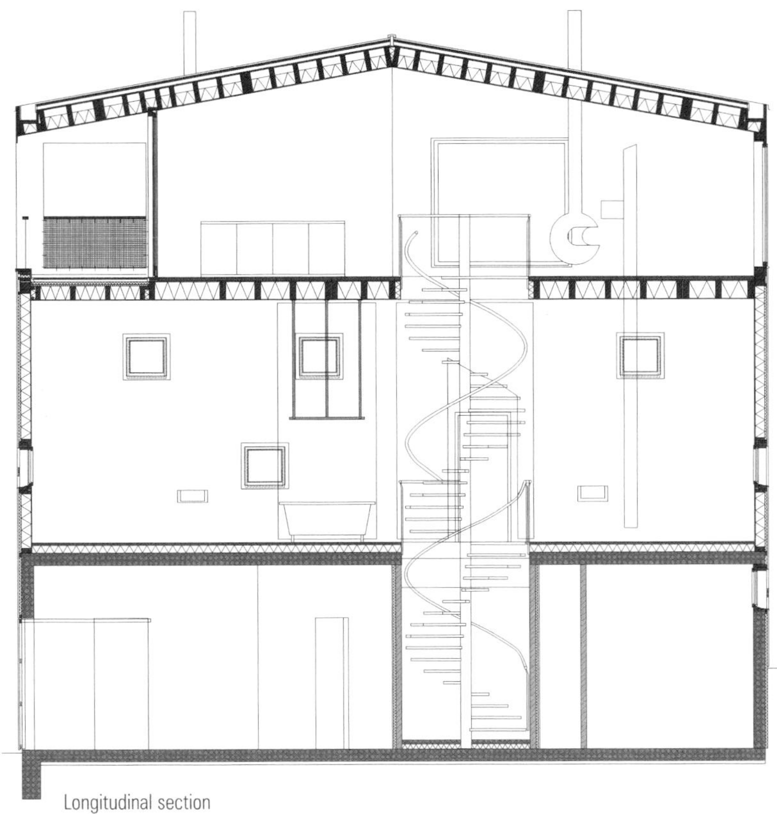

Longitudinal section

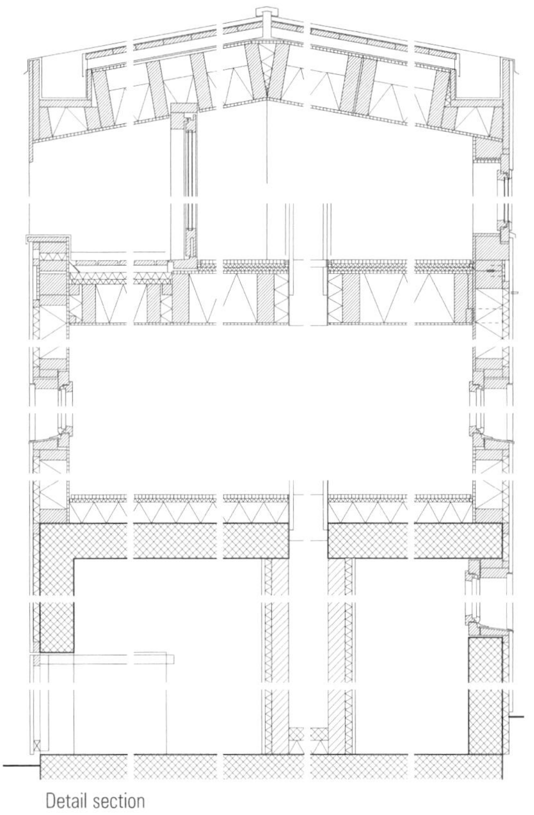

Detail section

Traut Architekten

Single Family House

Bad Camberg, Germany

In a mixed environment of private houses with pitched roofs, rows of terraced houses and some apartment buildings that recall the formal language of the post-war years, a definite geometry identifies this intervention. The choice of materials strengthens the statement: black firebrick for the façades and gabions of basaltic stone for the retaining walls in the garden. The zoning regulation ruled a one floor building, but the sloping plot allowed for an entirely habitable basement. The building rests on a slab of reinforced concrete. The outer and the inner walls are of lightweight concrete blocks between reinforced concrete supports. The roof is of reinforced concrete and concrete slab.

Plain materials typify the interior and the outdoors, and a brief repertoire of details helped to control the budget.

Facing the street, the building presents a wide glazed opening which frames the welcoming ruby red door. The main entrance is on the ground floor, where a curtain wall separates the living room from the hall and the kitchen. The lower level contains sleeping accommodation; light enters through the ample stairwell and the windows on the side; curtain walls separate various rooms.

With the two main openings oriented to catch the sunshine, this is an energy saving house. Unagressive materials have been chosen throughout, and a cistern gathers rainwater from the roof. A powerful hedge encloses the plot on the western side. The slope in the terrain has been transformed into a series of terraces with gabions of basaltic stone as retaining walls. Sets of parallel flowerbeds echo these lines and remind one of bar codes.

Photographs: Thomas Balzer

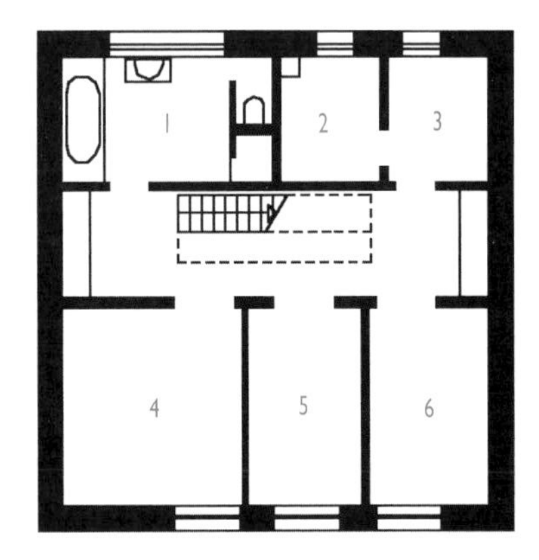

Basement

1. Bath
2. Technic
3. Store
4. Bedroom
5. Study
6. Bedroom

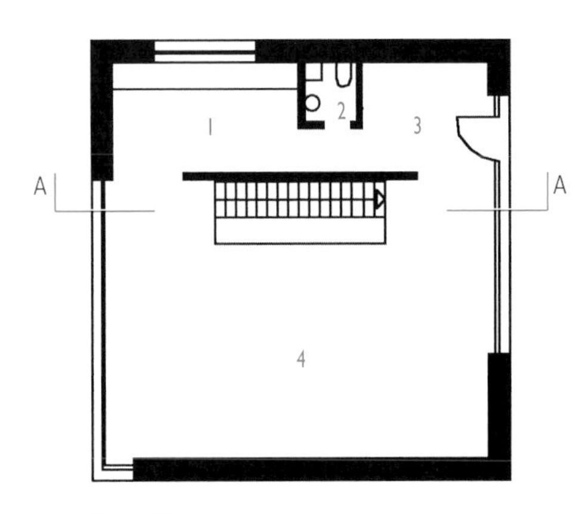

Ground Floor

1. Kitchen
2. WC
3. Entrance
4. Living and Dining

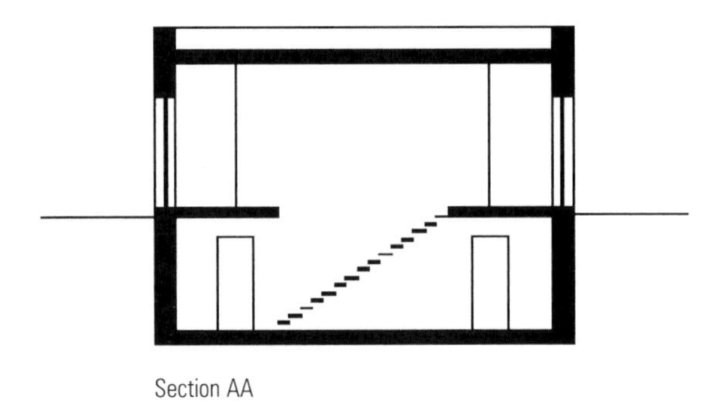

Section AA

This building is characterized by its rectilinear design and the austere materials used to build it: black fire brick for the facade and basaltic rock for the retaining wall. Urban planning regulations restrict buildings to a single floor, but the sloping site allowed a basement floor to be included as part of the living space.

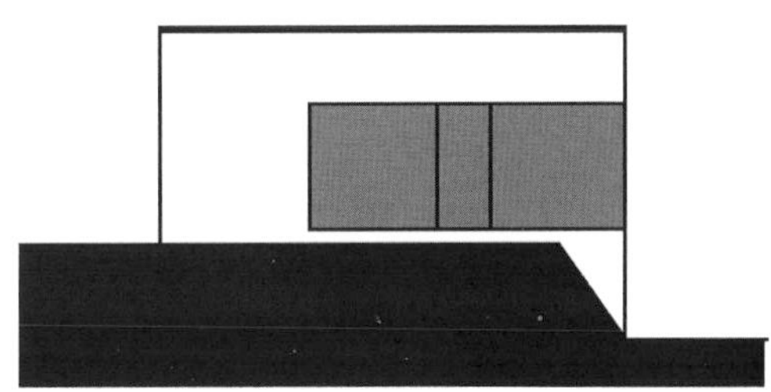

West Elevation

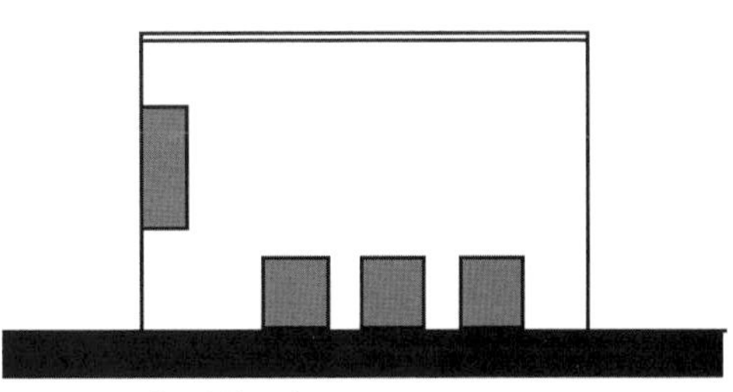

South Elevation

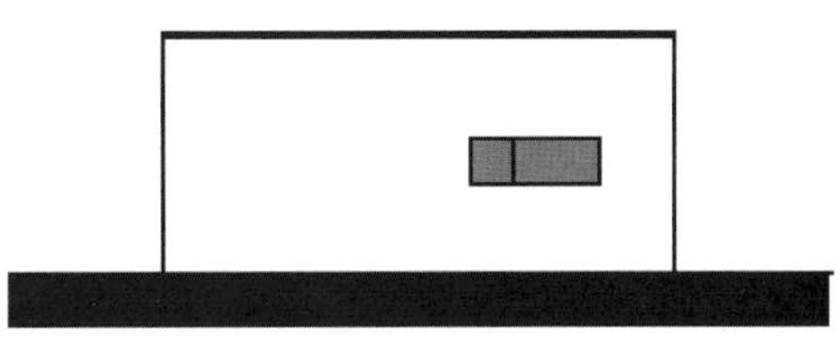

North Elevation

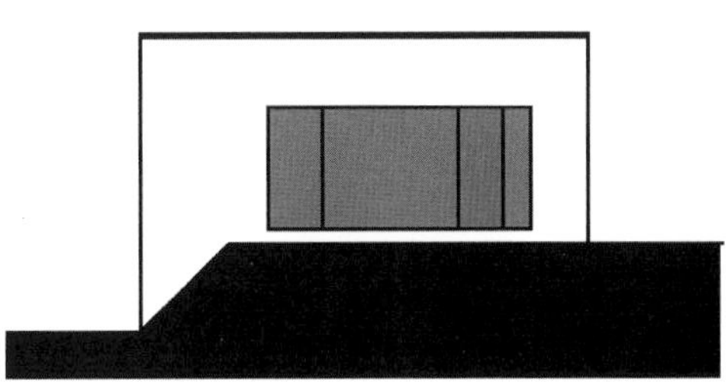

East Elevation

DRY design, inc.

3773 Studio

Los Angeles, USA

The project consists of a new 640 square-foot studio and bathroom, replacing an existing garage on a 45 x 115 foot site in Mar Vista, on the west side of Los Angeles. It was designed by John Jennings and Sasha Tarnopolsky of DRY design, inc. for their own home.
The building was designed in conjunction with a new backyard landscape. Behind its simple residential form there is an intricate program of spatial relationships, an interplay between space that is "loaded" at the periphery and the objects or figures within
The studio is comprised of a series of vertical trays. The lower tray is poured concrete and houses most of the functional areas. The middle tray is a plywood loft hung from the roof trusses. The upper tray, formed by the roof parapet, houses a roof deck and garden.

The building was designed as a home office or studio but can also be used as a separate living unit. The loft becomes a sleeping loft and the laundry doubles as a kitchen. A full bathroom, including indoor and outdoor showers, is accessed through two exterior doors. The bathroom reads externally as a separate volume, but also houses the kitchen bay. The loft is the same width as the kitchen bay, visually continuing the external volume of the bathroom all the way through the interior of the studio. Adjacent volumes exert pressure on each other that can be read internally through the diagonal wall and the continuous joists that run through the wall supporting the bathroom roof on one side, and the hung loft on the other.

Photographs: Undine Pröhl

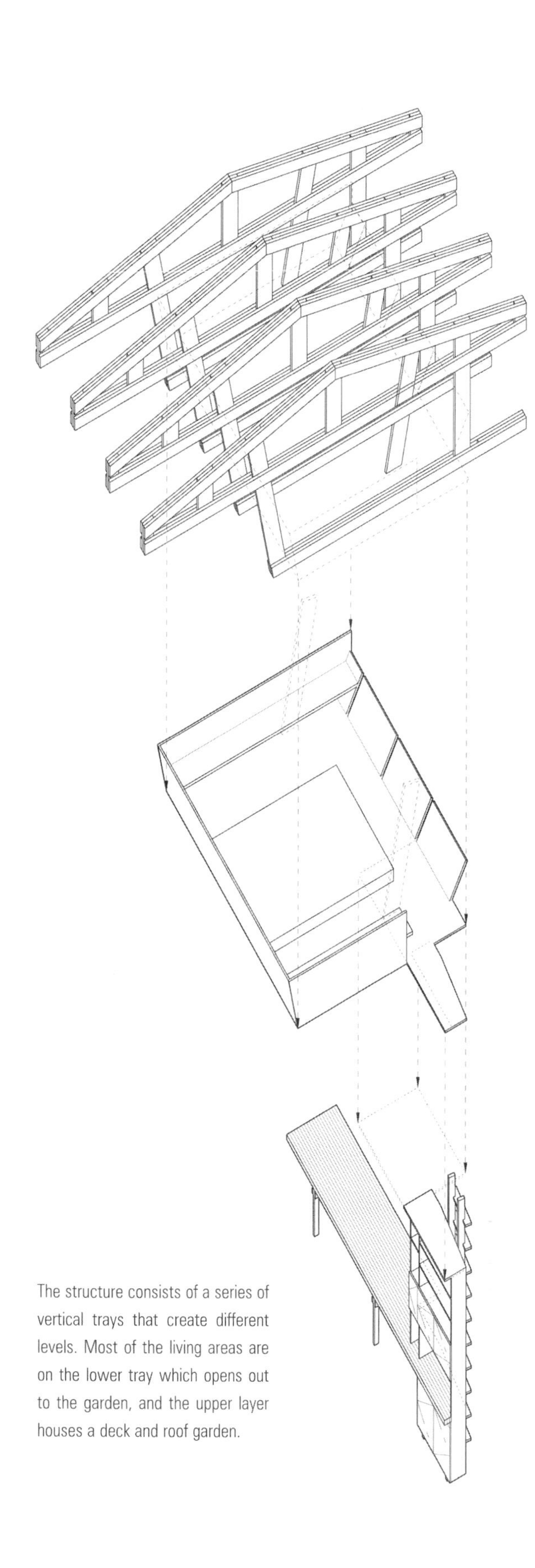

The structure consists of a series of vertical trays that create different levels. Most of the living areas are on the lower tray which opens out to the garden, and the upper layer houses a deck and roof garden.

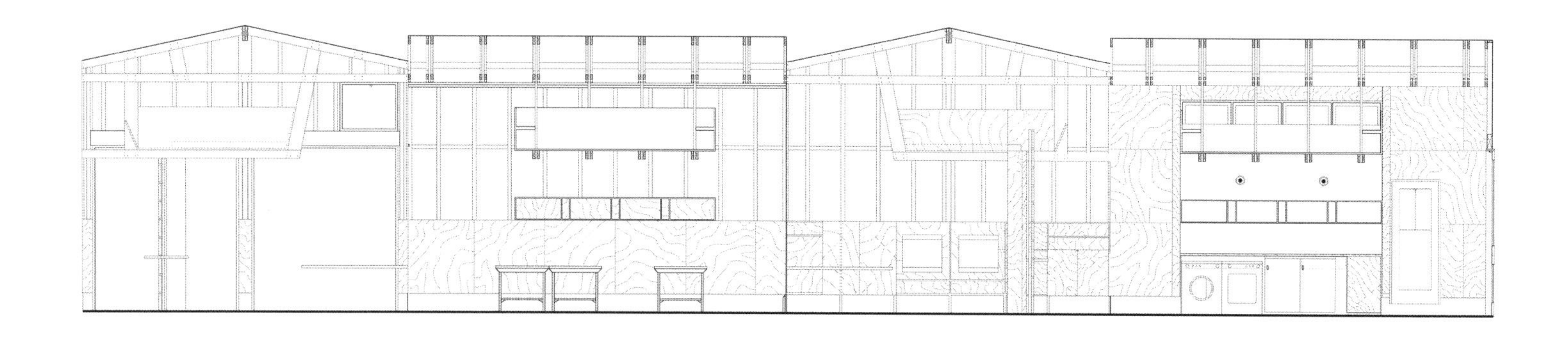

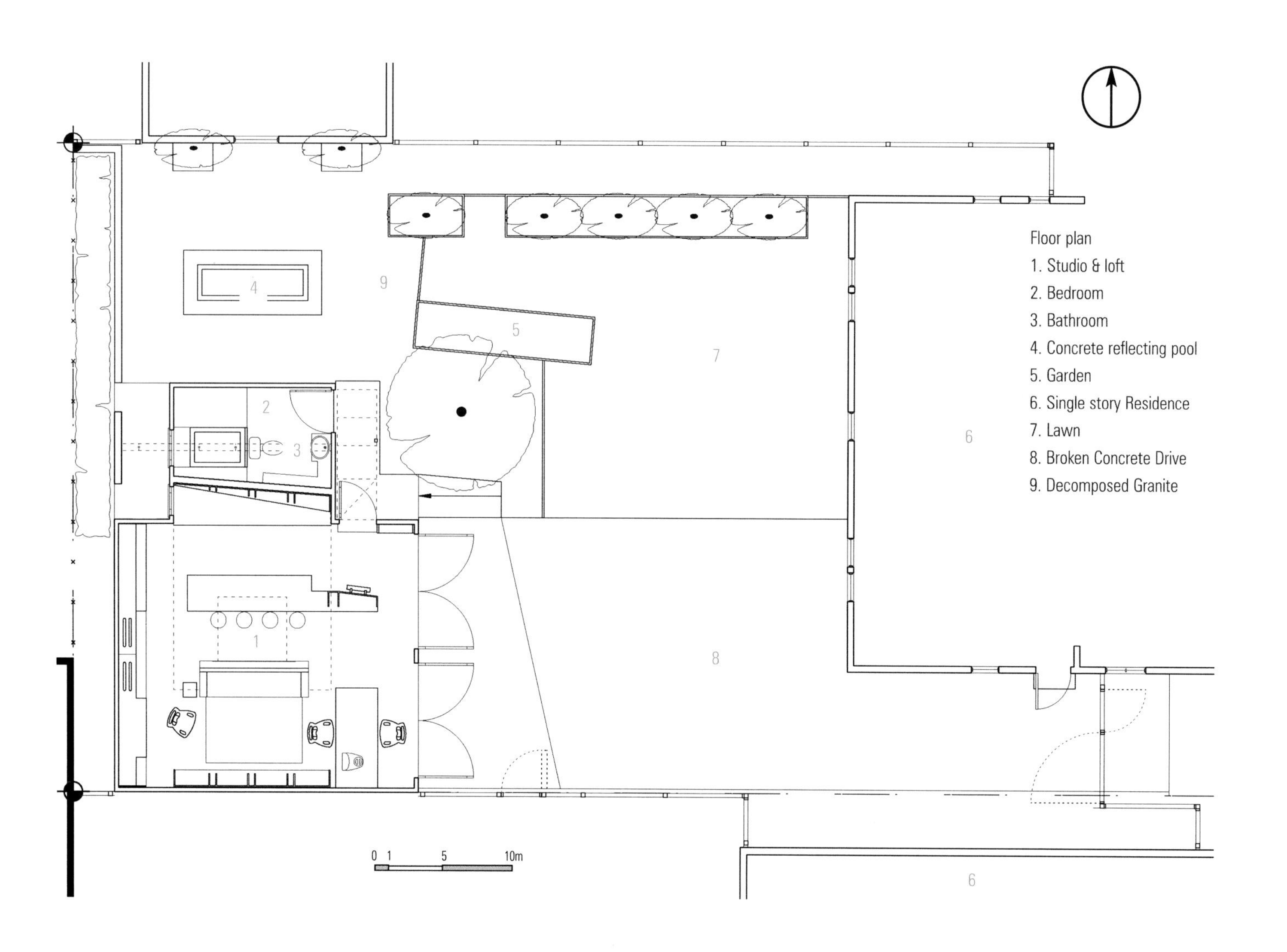

Floor plan
1. Studio & loft
2. Bedroom
3. Bathroom
4. Concrete reflecting pool
5. Garden
6. Single story Residence
7. Lawn
8. Broken Concrete Drive
9. Decomposed Granite
0 1 5 10m

JOHN LE CARRÉ
THE CONSTANT GARDENER
DIAMOND
MATTHEW HART

Jun Aoki

House I

Tokyo, Japan

The most has been made of this relatively small plot. Of the 61 m^2 of available ground space, a two-story home with a basement has been built on just 37 m^2 (the total floor area is 109 m^2). However, its impact on the surrounding neighborhood cannot be judged by its size alone. The eye-catching and unexpected geometry of the facade sets this home apart from the rest.

The project is a sculpted concrete shell placed in the space between two existing houses. Broadly speaking, the structure is comprised of two independent volumes placed within the shell. The upper floor, from which is seemingly suspended a glass-enclosed mezzanine overlooking the dining room, comprise the first volume; the second is made up of the ground floor, which encloses the basement space.

The primary structural system is of reinforced concrete. The facades are clad in wood paneling, with windows framed in aluminum and steel.

In the interior, the sleek, modern look of steel and concrete competes with the homey warmth of wood. High and wide expanses of exposed concrete slabs make an imposing wall cladding. The floors are done almost entirely in unstained wood throughout the home, the only exception being the unique flooring material used in the mezzanine: leather.

Painted steel stairways and handrails, and custom-designed steel cabinets are the elements which provide the necessary dark visual counterweight to the light tones of concrete and unstained wood.

Photographs: Tsunejiro Watanabe

Ground floor plan

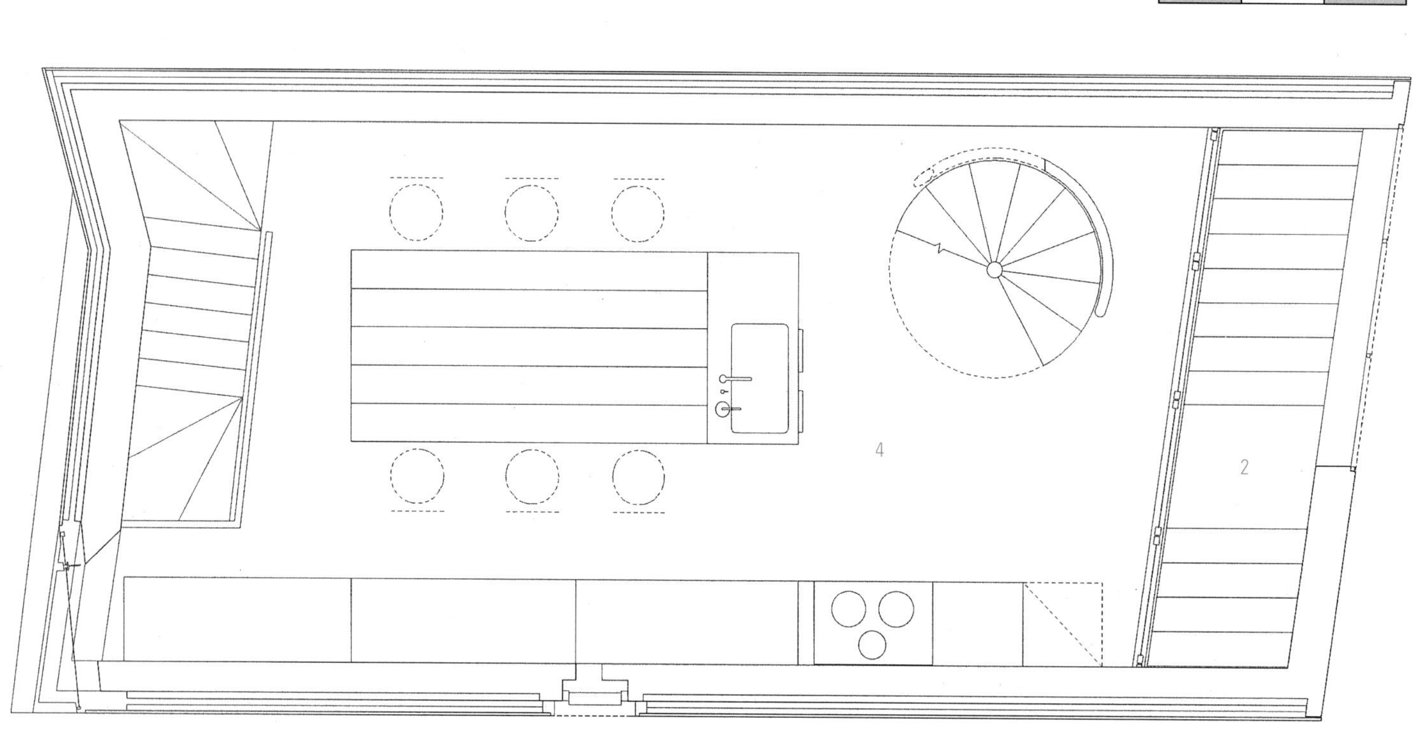

First floor plan

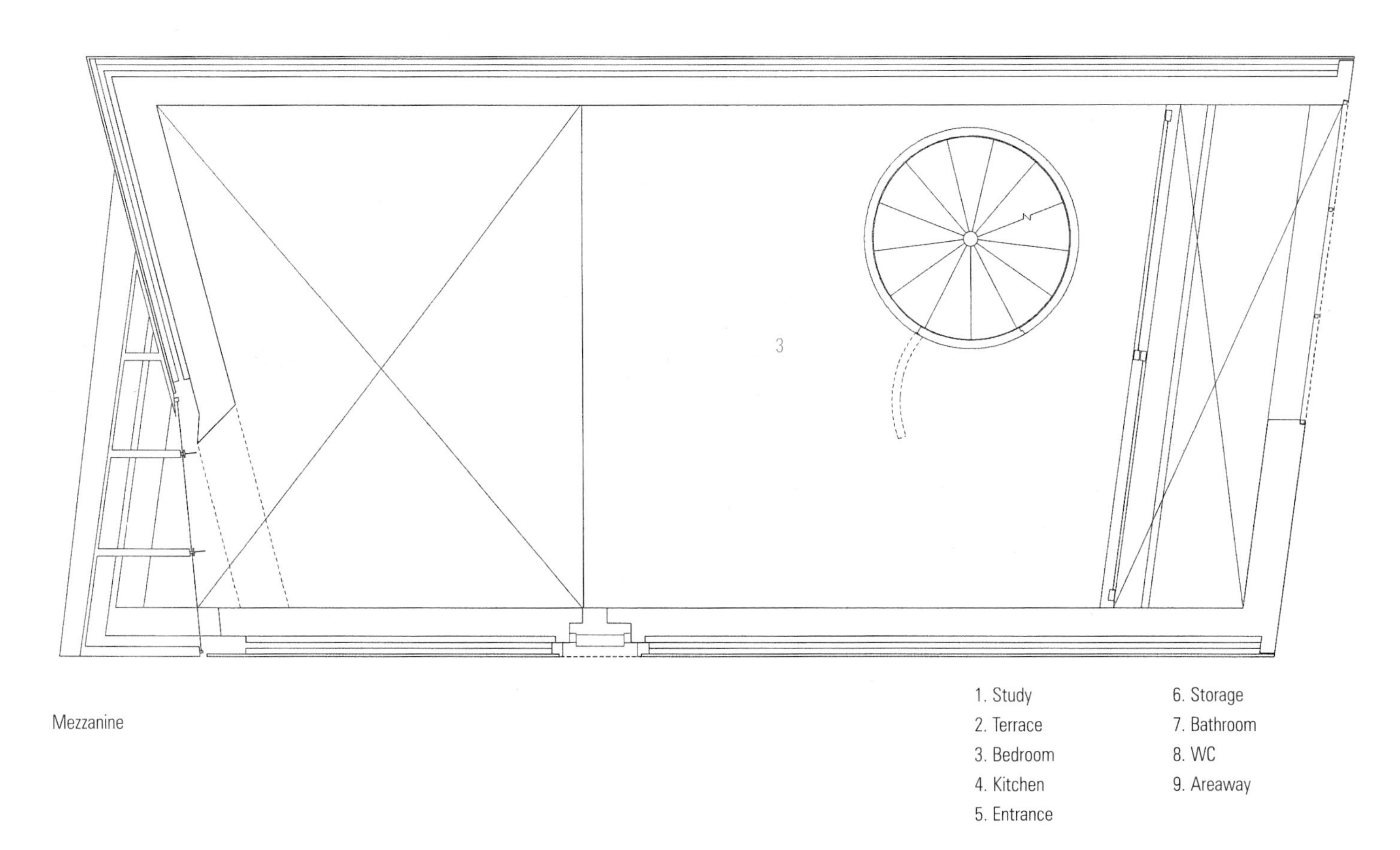

Mezzanine

1. Study
2. Terrace
3. Bedroom
4. Kitchen
5. Entrance
6. Storage
7. Bathroom
8. WC
9. Areaway

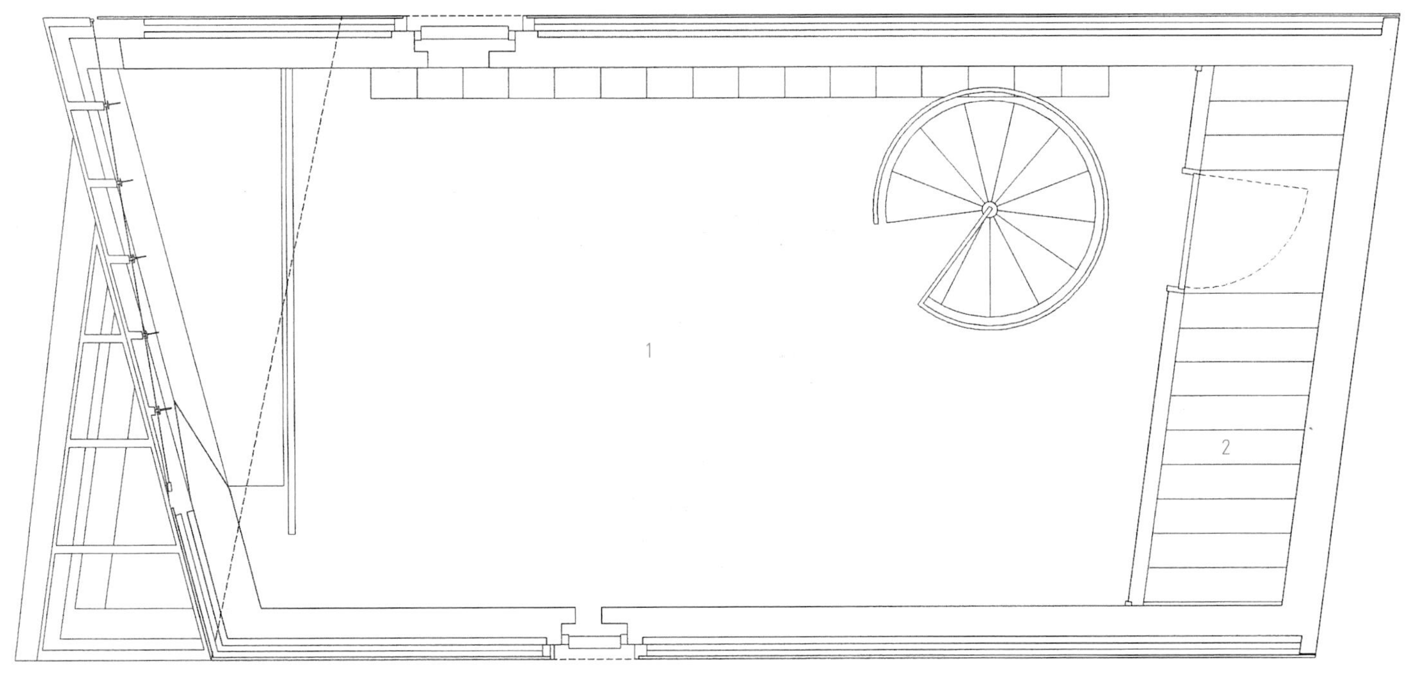

Second floor plan

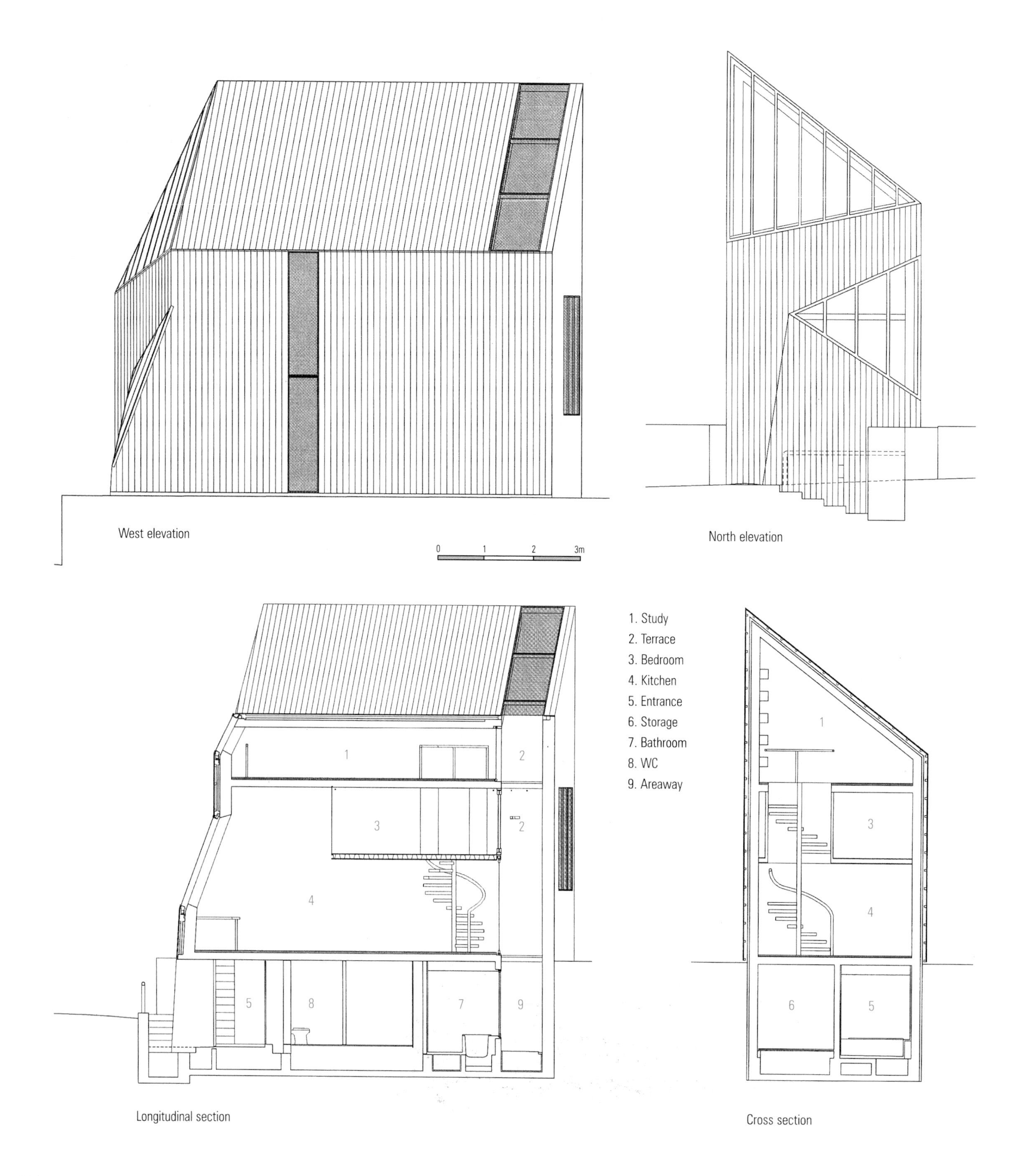
West elevation
0
1
2
3m
North elevation
1. Study
2. Terrace
3. Bedroom
4. Kitchen
5. Entrance
6. Storage
7. Bathroom
8. WC
9. Areaway
1
2
3
2
4
5
8
7
9
1
3
4
6
5
Longitudinal section
Cross section

The walls are clad in high and wide expanses of exposed concrete. The floors are done almost entirely in unstained wood, the only exception being the unique flooring material used in the mezzanine: leather.

Thinking Space Architects

House on Club Row London

London, UK

This house had been a vacant site since the four-story building previously occupying the site (built in 1840) was demolished in 1957. It is surrounded on three boundaries by existing structures. To the north is a substantial three-story warehouse building with smaller, converted two- and three-story residential buildings to the east and south. These smaller buildings have windows facing the boundaries, and there is an existing right of way for a fire escape running across the site. These constraints, combined with limited space (62 sq m), meant that the property had been passed over by developers, and was deemed unusable for anything other than a parking lot.
The house aims to participate in the street and draw on its generosity. For this reason the house is highly glazed and open on the main street elevation. The Georgian houses on the adjacent street were an important precedent with their simple geometry and large openings. To overcome the lack of external views and height restrictions imposed by zoning laws, an atrium plan was developed. This creates quiet, secluded bedrooms (the street is on a bus route), stacked at the rear of the house on the ground and first floors, with a sequence of more public living spaces rising from the basement to the roof terrace. On the north side a service zone is generated by the stair well, which provides storage and areas for the kitchen and showers.
This simple design scheme creates clear volumes which are linked and dramatically lit by the atrium allowing all the rooms to participate in this south-facing home, with its sensation of spaciousness in a relatively limited space.
The basement acts as a raft foundation, removing the need for deep foundations with the stub spine walls at the front and, adjacent to the stairs, strengthening the existing party wall and providing cross bracing to the structure.

Photographs: Edmund Sumner

The bedrooms can take ventilation either from the atrium in winter or directly from the outside in summer. Windows have been fitted with low E glass panes, with steel frames abd movable, insulated, hardwood ventilation panels. This house has been designed to be energy efficient, while at the same time open to the exterior as much as possible.

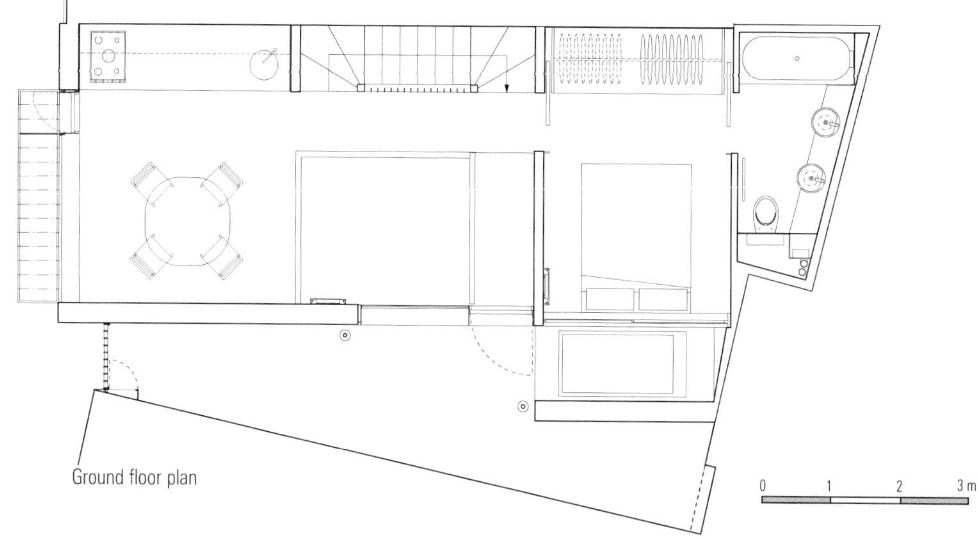

Ground floor plan

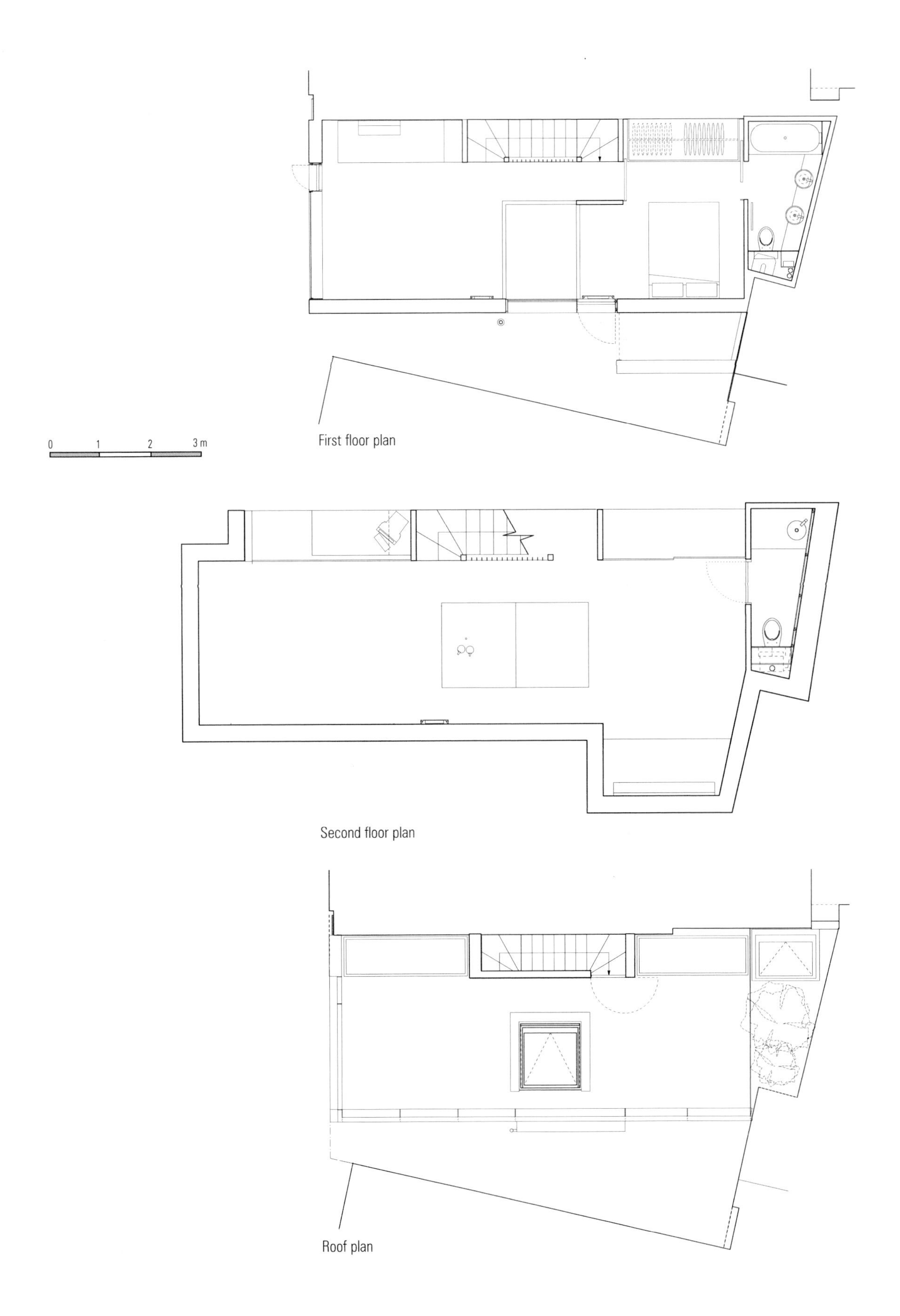

First floor plan

Second floor plan

Roof plan

Elevation to main street

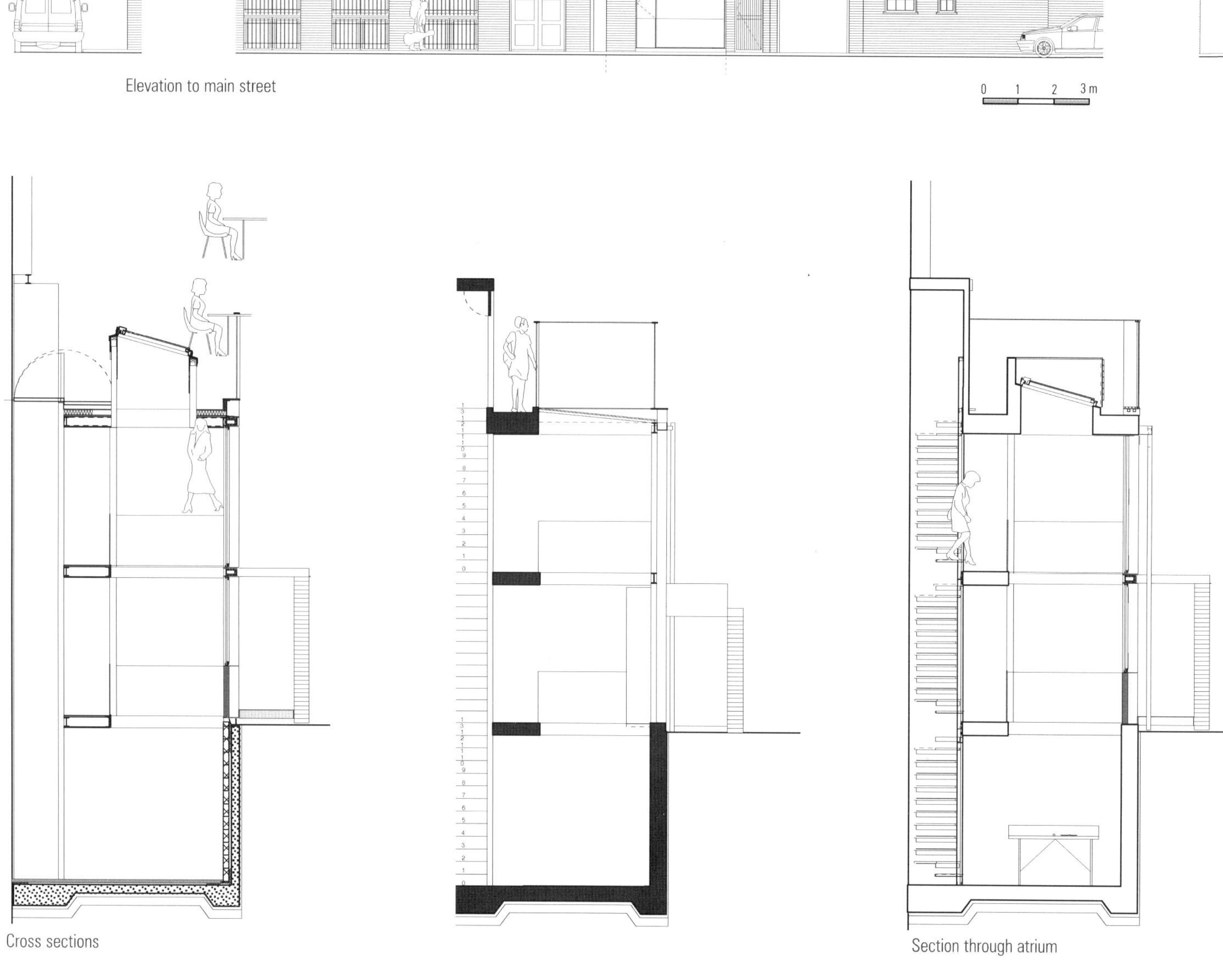
Cross sections

Section through atrium

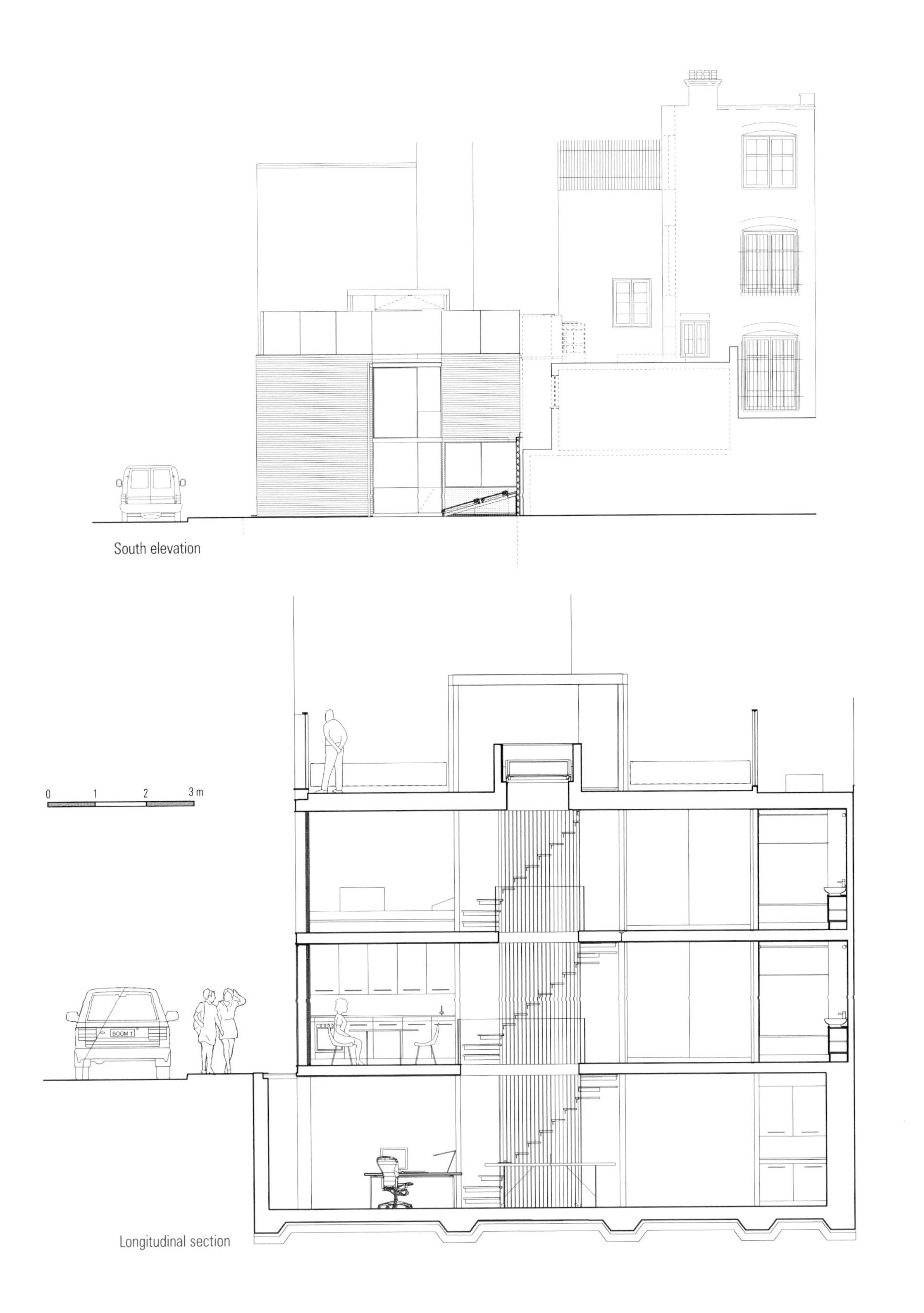

South elevation

Longitudinal section

The superstructure is simple, consisting of planes of well insulated cavity masonry walls with wood and steel floor plates. This sturdy construction is combined with a relatively sophisticated services installation consisting of a condensing boiler, which provides under-floor heating with heat reclaim ducted ventilation to the bedrooms and bathrooms.

Tomotsugu Akutsu Architects

House in Minaminasu

Tochigi, Japan

This house was built for a couple and their child in a grain-producing region in the north part of the Kanto Plain, about 100 kilometers from Tokyo. The 500m site is on an old wheat field, which was redeveloped for housing use using land fill.

As the site is large enough, a single-story structure was chosen. A traditional Japanese dimension, four and a half straw mats, which is equivalent to a 2.73 m^2, was adopted as a module for the layout. A grid of four units by four units was laid out to organize the interior space.

One of the features of the house is that there are two living rooms and two entrances, one for guests and one for family use. This allows the family to keep an area for entertaining in the traditional way, apart from the spaces that tend to get filled by the modern accumulation of goods in contemporary Japanese living.

Each of the rooms in the house is gently connected by three sliding doors. When these doors are opened, all the rooms join to create one large room. When they are closed, each space can be used as a small room. In this way, the design is flexible and can be used for many purposes.

Exterior features such as the elevated floor, external wood wall and uncovered pillars reflect the features of traditional houses of the region, reinterpreted in a modern style.

Photographs: Kaori Ichikawa

The construction materials and structure of the building are based on the traditional houses of the area. The elevated floor, wood wall, pillars and the dimensions of the house are traditional features reinterpreted in a modern style.

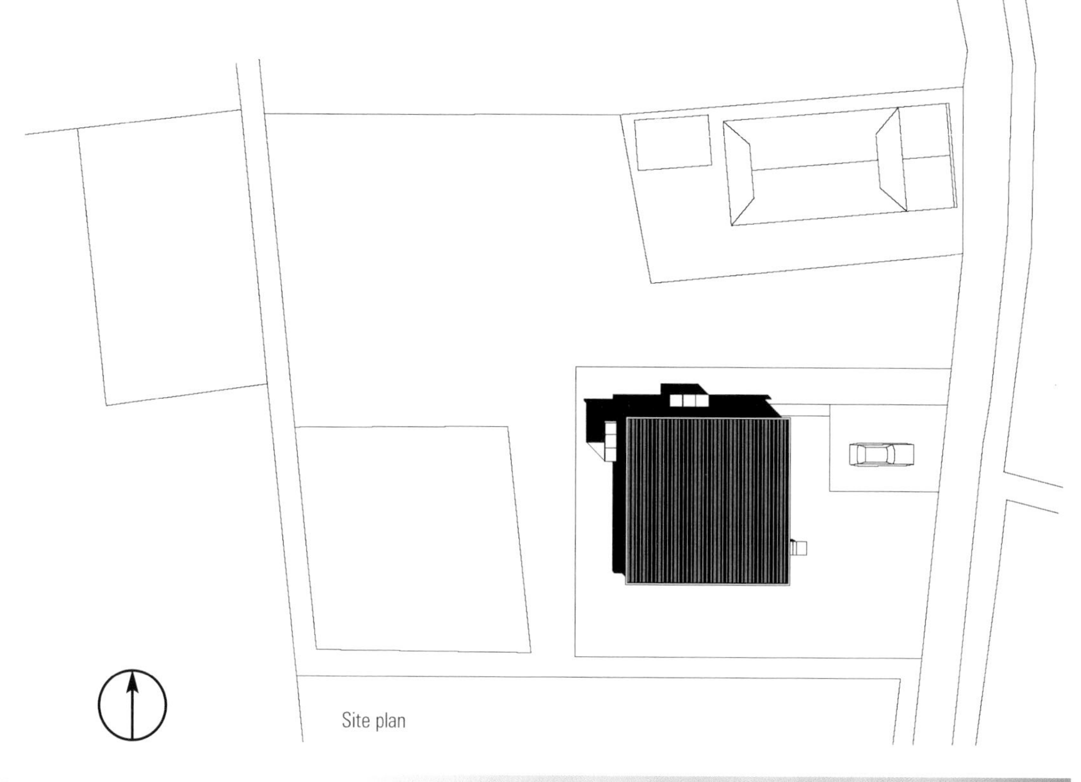

Site plan

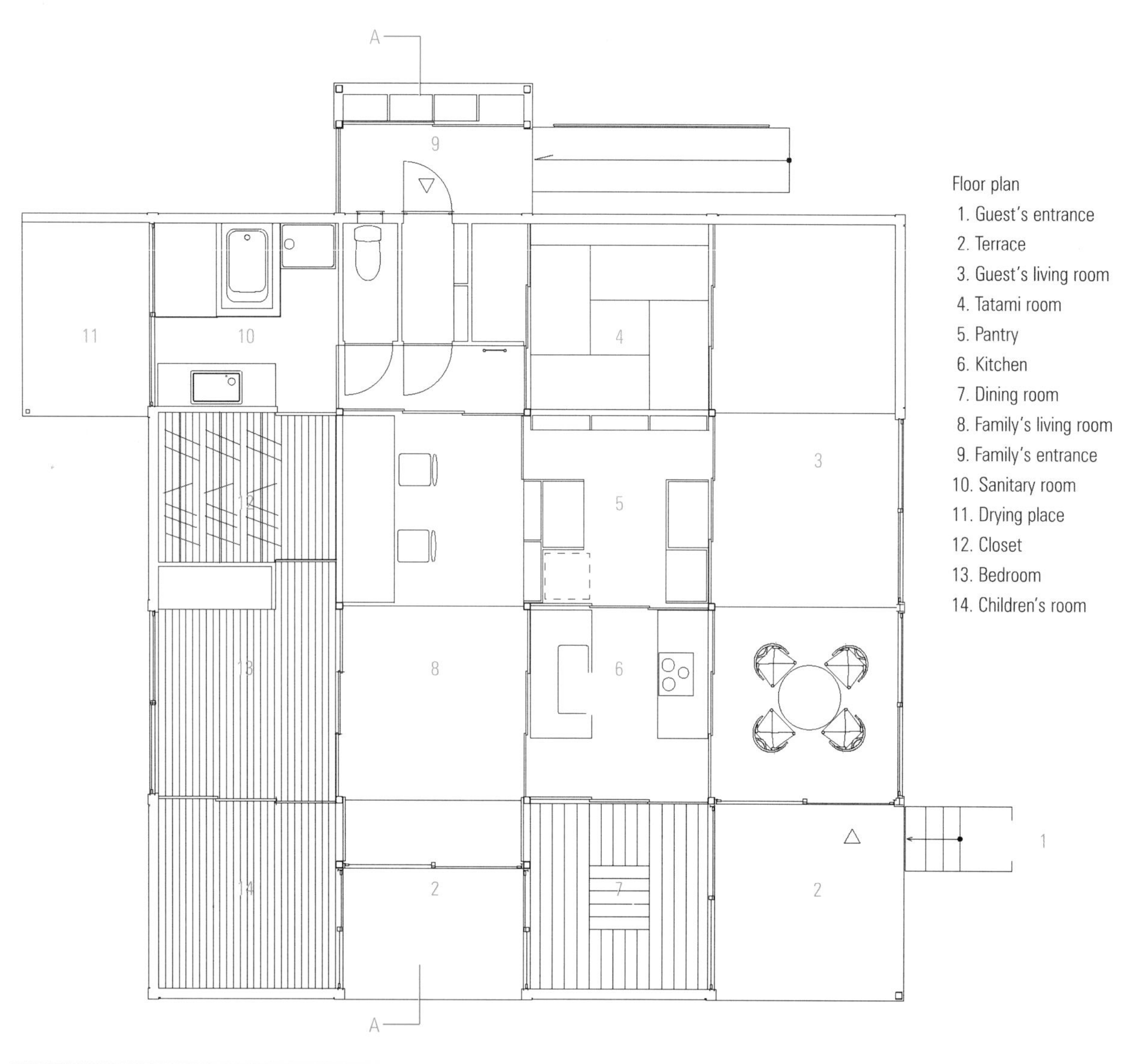

Floor plan

1. Guest's entrance
2. Terrace
3. Guest's living room
4. Tatami room
5. Pantry
6. Kitchen
7. Dining room
8. Family's living room
9. Family's entrance
10. Sanitary room
11. Drying place
12. Closet
13. Bedroom
14. Children's room

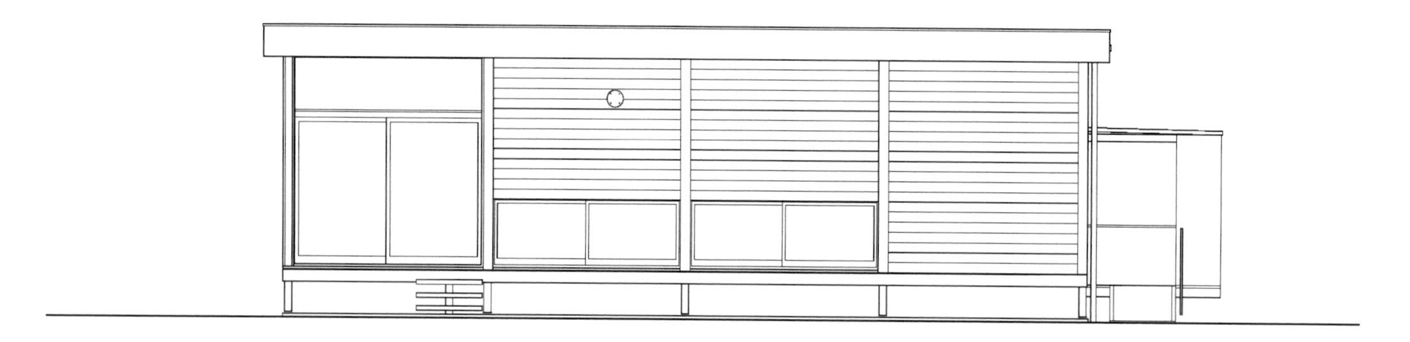

East elevation

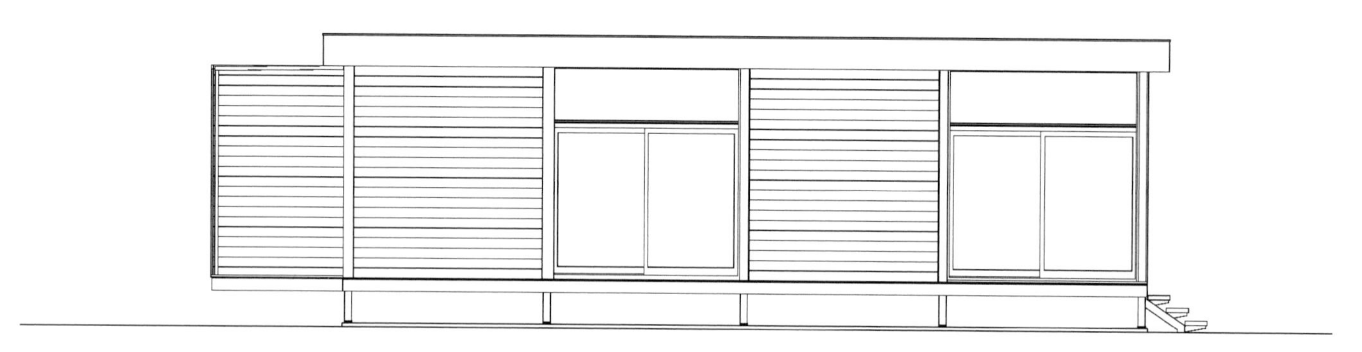

South elevation

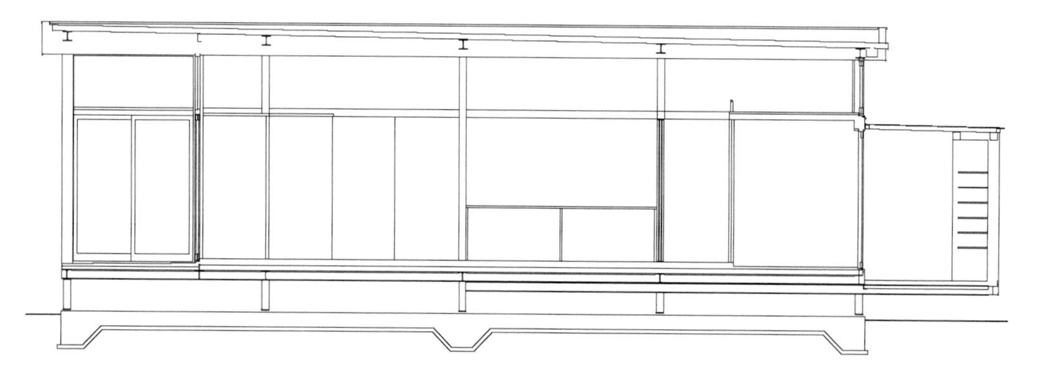

Section AA

The weeHouse team / Warner + Asmus

weeHouse

Minnesota, USA

The motivation behind the pared down design of this house was a rejection of the trend in the US that bigger is better. The weeHouse, designed for Stephani Arado by Geoff Warner of Minnesota-based Alchemy Architects, is a study in efficient use of space. The contemporary cabin is a simple 12-foot by 24-foot rectangle with glass sides. It contains custom cabinetry, cantilevered shelves with sliding aluminum doors and two built-in beds. The weeHouse was built in response to Arado's limited budget, her desire to minimally impact the site, and to create a quiet space for retreat. The quality of space was more important than amenities (there is no electricity, running water, or sewer connection). It serves as a weekend getaway and is essentially a log cabin in the country. The location, a small plot on Minnesota farmland, was remote and lacking in basic facilities, so the house was prefabricated and transported whole. Instead of contracting out the work, Warner built the cabin himself, with the help of Lucas Alm and Scott McGlasson, both of whom share Warner's Minnesota office. The cabin took about eight weeks to complete, was trucked to the site, and hoisted onto its foundation by crane.

Photographs: Warner + Asmus

STOP

The cabin is singular in style because of its simplicity, construction method and the fact that it was designed for its site. The weeHouse is Arado's prefabricated sanctuary, the place she goes whenever she wants to be peaceful.

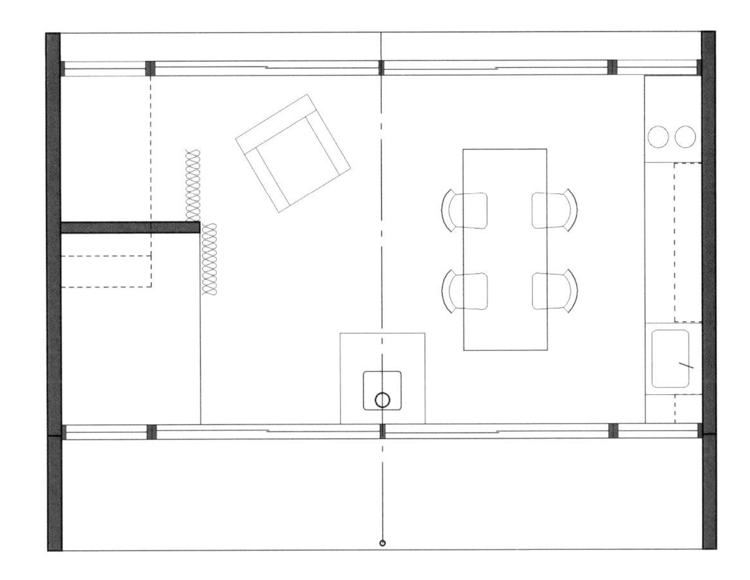

The floor plan is extremely simple: a 3.60x7.25 m rectangle with enough space for a kitchen and two beds placed against the wall. The rest of the furniture consists of made-to-measure wardrobes, projecting shelves with aluminum doors, a table for four and the chimney.

OPD

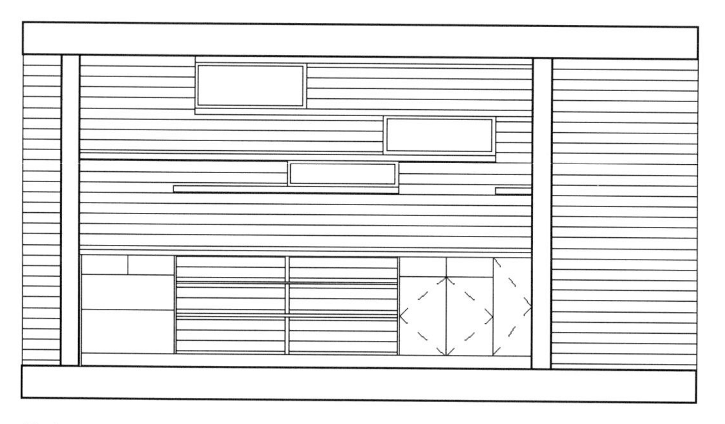

Kitchen elevation

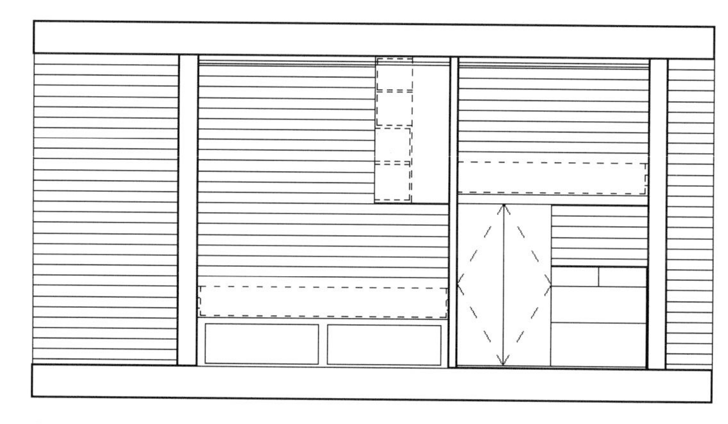

Bedroom elevation

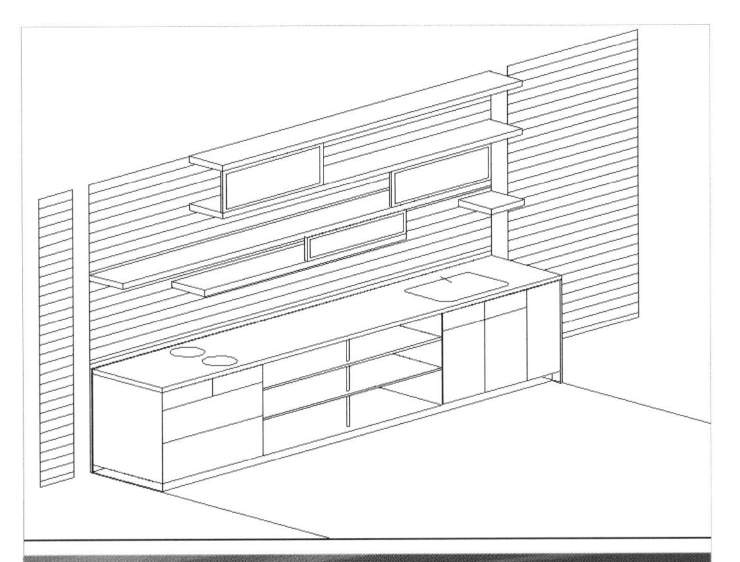

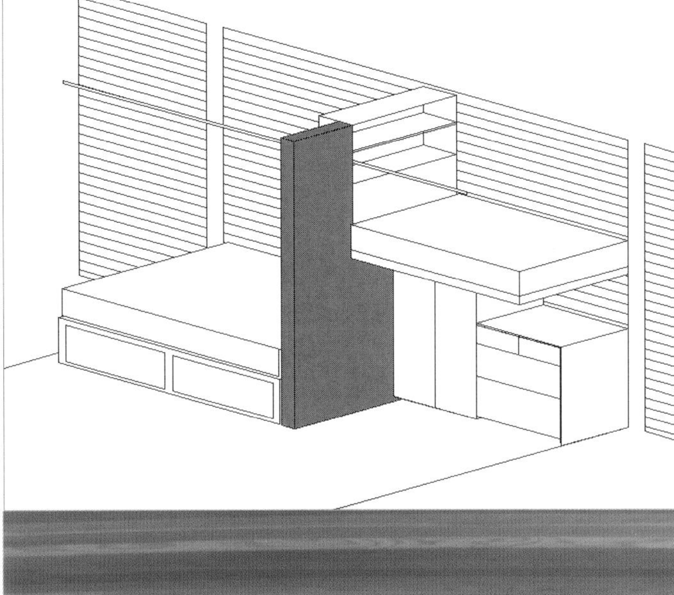

Takaharu + Yui Tezuka / Tezuka Architects, Masahiro Ikeda / mias

House to catch the sky III

Saitama, Japan

The site is located in a suburban area of Tokyo that was recently developed from farmland into residential lots of approximately one hundred square meters. The neighborhood is characterized by brand-new, two-storey wooden houses which are being built in a variety of colors. Sooner or later the site itself will be surrounded by similar buildings on three sides, but otherwise nothing particular emerges from the context.

If one followed the example of other constructions in the area, a two-storey house built near the northern edge of the lot would leave virtually no space for a garden. On the other hand, a single-storey structure would be dominated by the neighboring houses, and left without much light. Large windows on the southern façade would be no answer either, since curtains would have to be shut at all times to ensure privacy.

The surface of the site is roughly 148.5 meters square. A 60 percent building-to-land ratio would leave nearly 90 square meters for a single-storey house, the equivalent of a two-storey house with 115 square meters. Such a space would provide enough room to accommodate a married couple. The structure of the House to Catch the Sky III was designed very simply: a square box with a central light well that was created by cutting and lowering a rectangular portion of the roof above the core. The sky is the only direction towards which both a certain privacy and space can be guaranteed in Japanese urban areas. The high-side opening was thus designed to circumscribe the view to the sky and the roofs of surrounding buildings. In this way privacy does not become a matter of concern, and the sunlight can penetrate the house equally throughout the day.

Photographs: Katsuhisa Kida

Measuring approximately 150 m², the plot is set on the outskirts of Tokyo in an area that had once been used as farmland, but which has recently become populated with residential plots occupied by new, two-story wooden houses.

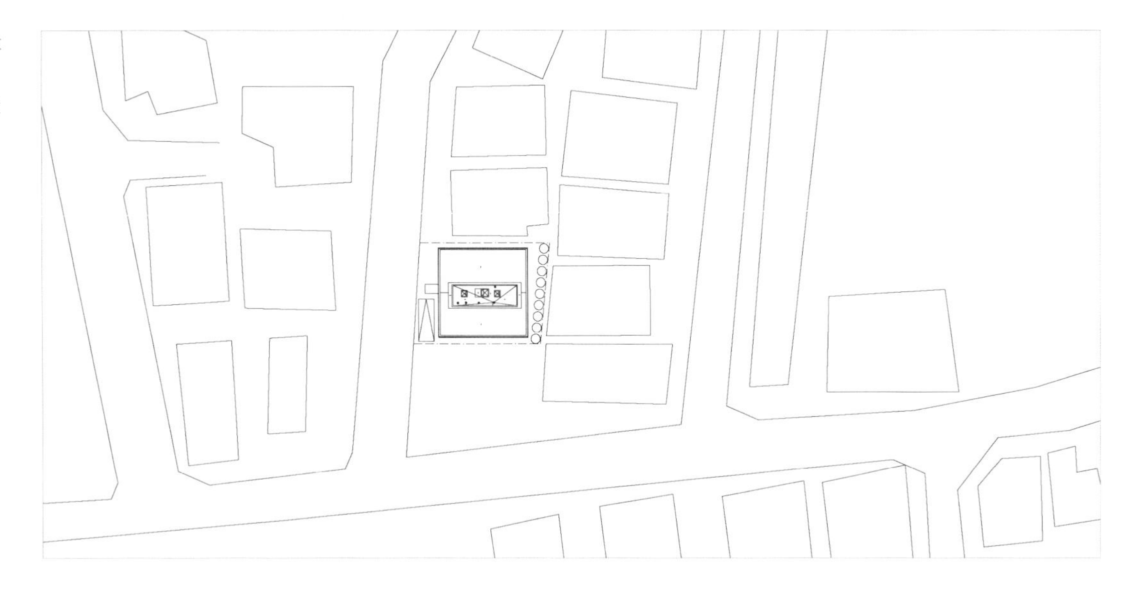

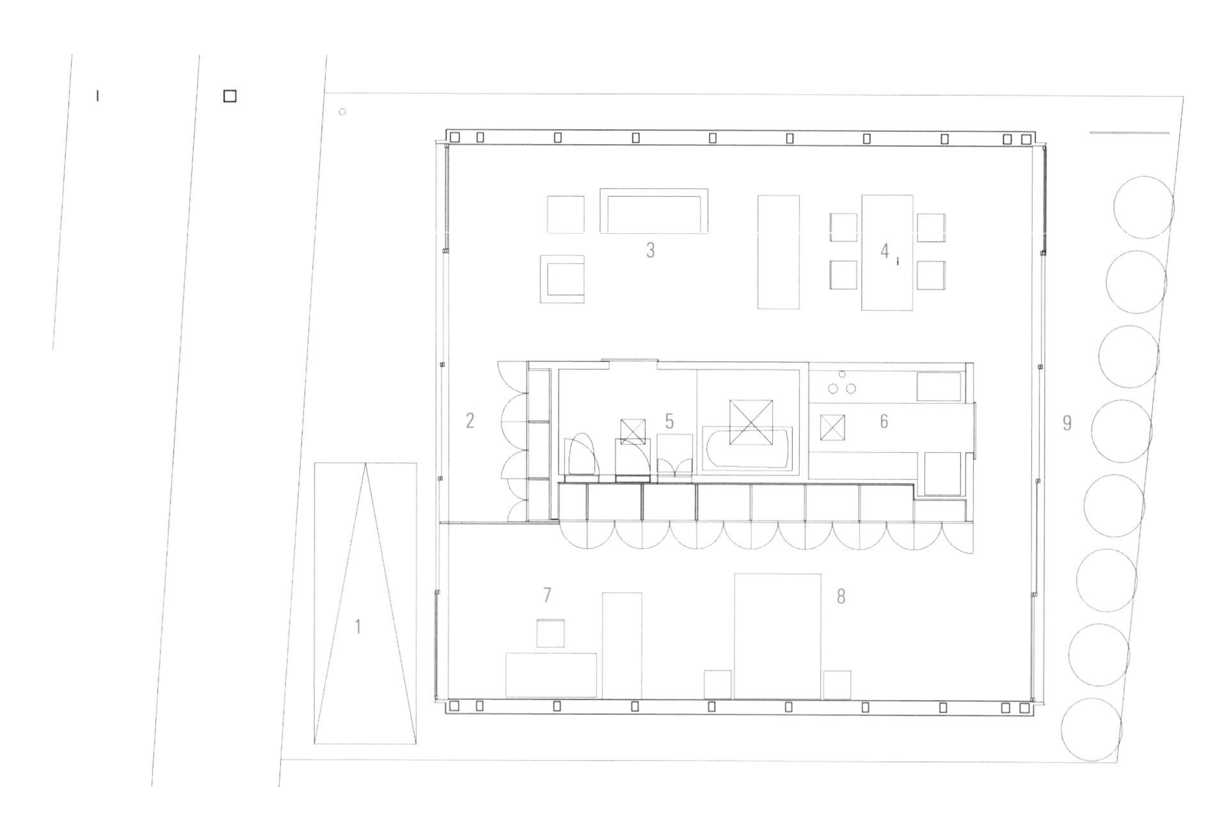

Floor plan
1. Parking
2. Entrance
3. Living room
4. Dining room
5. Bathroom
6. Kitchen
7. Office
8. Bedroom
9. Yard

Longitudinal section

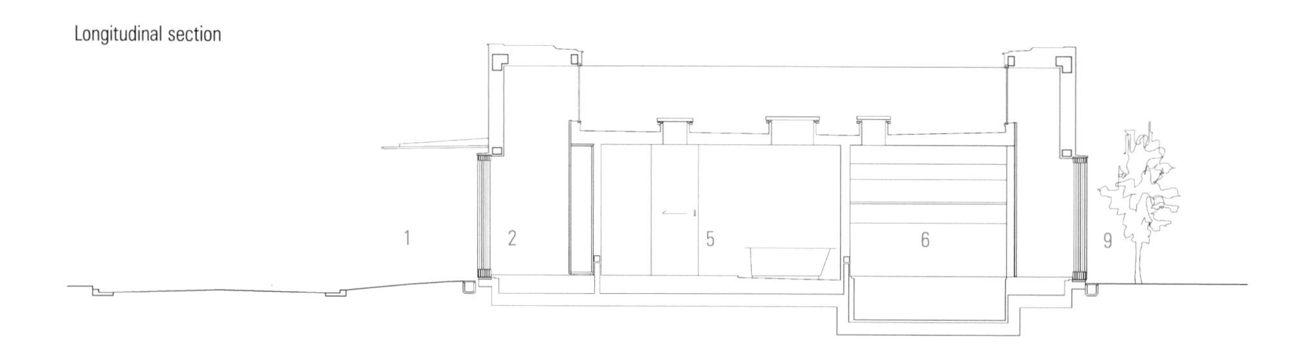

PIAA

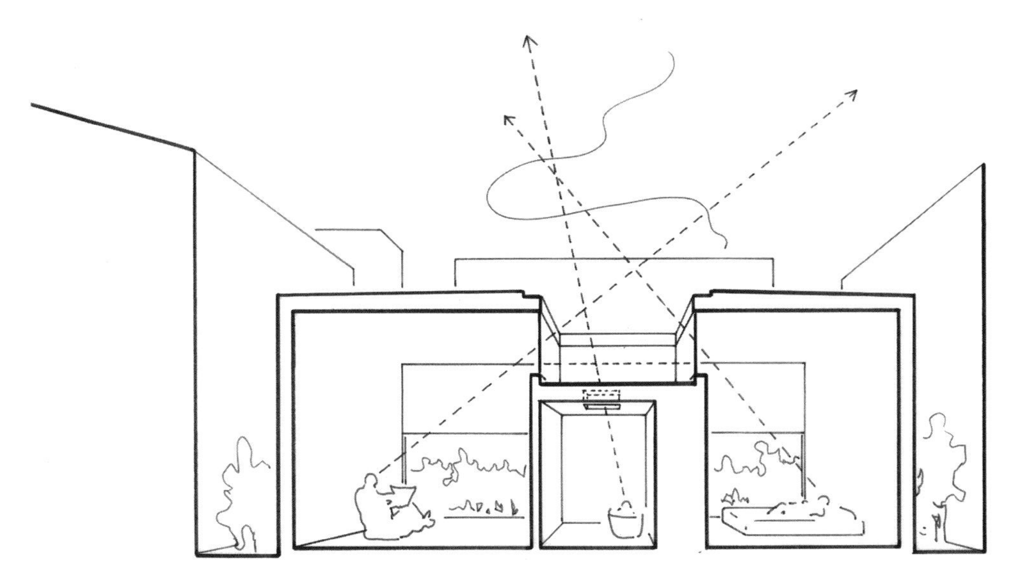

With a flat roof 3.2 meters above ground, the height of the building stands well within regulations. The whole structure is actually one single volume, with a bedroom and a living room occupying two equal spaces on both sides of the core, which contains the water storage systems.

G. Hamonic et J.C. Masson

House in a Garage

Paris, France

When a couple with children who are fond of ample space and contemporary design decide to free themselves from the corset of a Haussman building in Paris and are allergic to ready-to-wear real estate, they must take a decision on architecture. And with the same impetus they must offer the project to young designers. In life, the success of a project is often a question of confidence.

The chain that was established during this operation between the customer, the architect and the contractor is the illustration of this. Conquered from nothing, or almost nothing, this domestic dwelling was created from scratch from the first sketch to handover in a full year. The investment of the architects was proportionate to the confidence that the customers placed in them.

And this is how this old shell opening onto a passage on the outskirts of the old section of Paris became the mansion of their dreams. The scheme was not, strictly speaking, a rehabilitation but a more radical intervention, a way of making full use of the plot.

Two different environments are woven together: on the passage side, the old houses are preserved, with their roofing and their loft. In the heart of the block, in the place of the old hangar, the fluid space of the new intervention expands. Preserving its original character, the facade on the dead-end is almost unaltered. This choice of discretion and respect for the surrounding fabric that was desired from the first drawings by the architects helped the inhabitants of this modest dead-end of old Paris to accept the scheme.

On crossing the threshold, the visitor is inhaled toward a large, extremely open volume (the living room), which opens onto the court. The scenario of daily life is thus discovered. It forms a continuous whole of which full use is made, and life moves into the hollows of the works. The different spaces are linked by the interplay of light and the contrast of volumes. No doors, no obstacles. Transitions take the form of delicate filters: a bamboo hedge in the court, a set of transparent or translucent polycarbonate screens for the kitchen, dining area, lounge and offices.

Photographs: Hervé Abbadie / Hamonic + Masson Architectes

The house takes the old dimensions of the shell (192 m² floor space, 6 m height to the base of the roof), crossed by a court (3 m x 6 m) that regulates the party wall facing the court with a light partition. The 18 m² of space planted with bamboo becomes a garden, a source of light and a horizon of vegetation for all the rooms.

Site plan

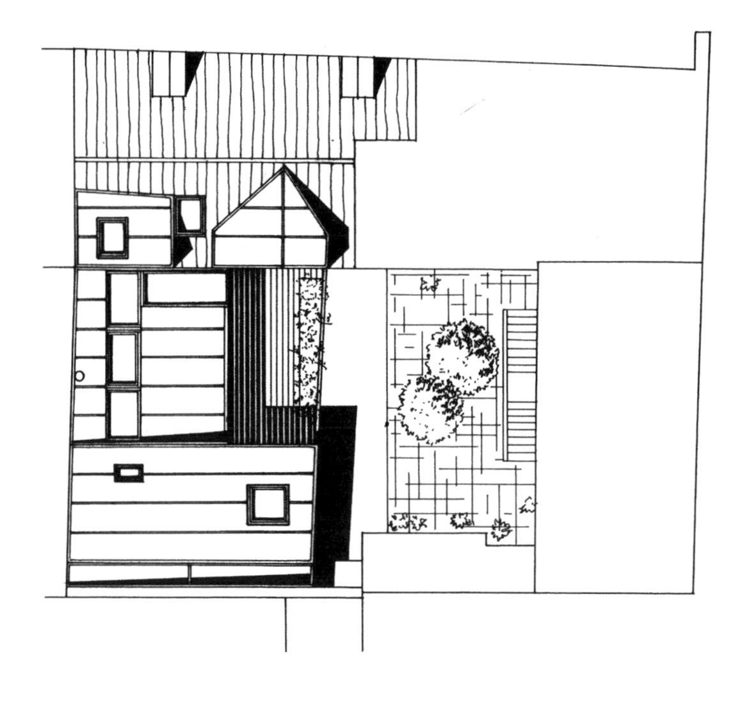

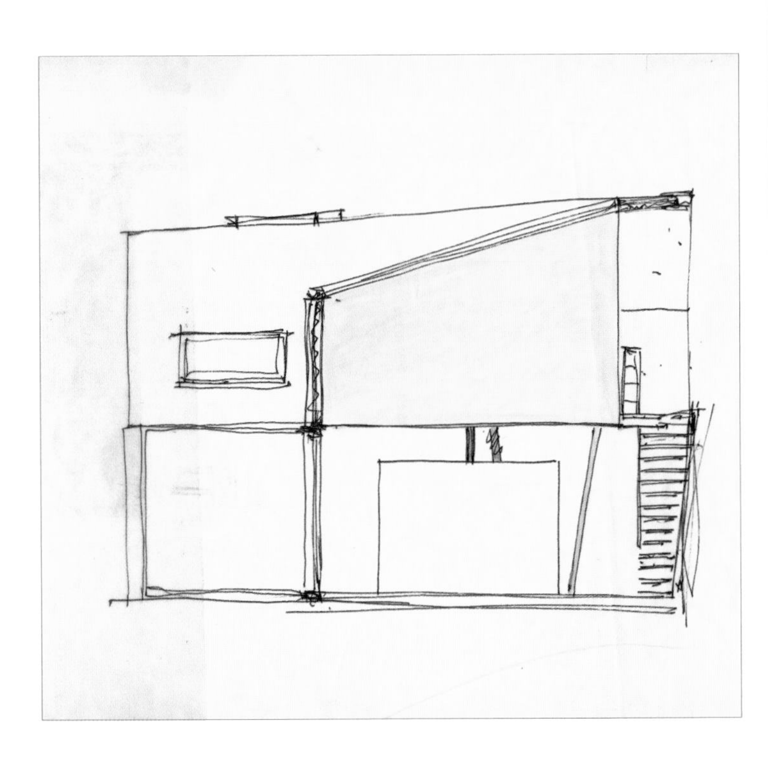

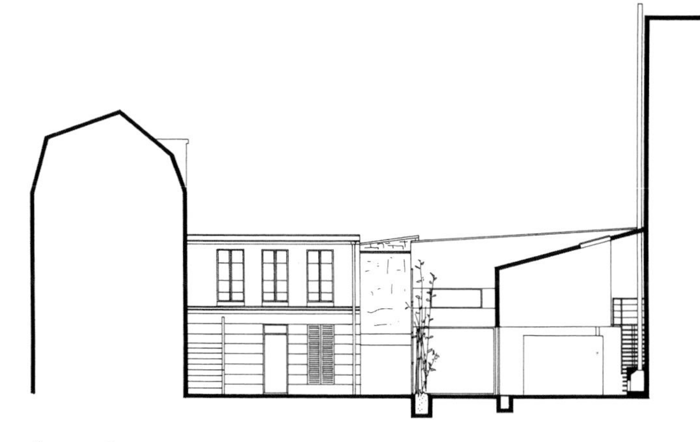

Cross section

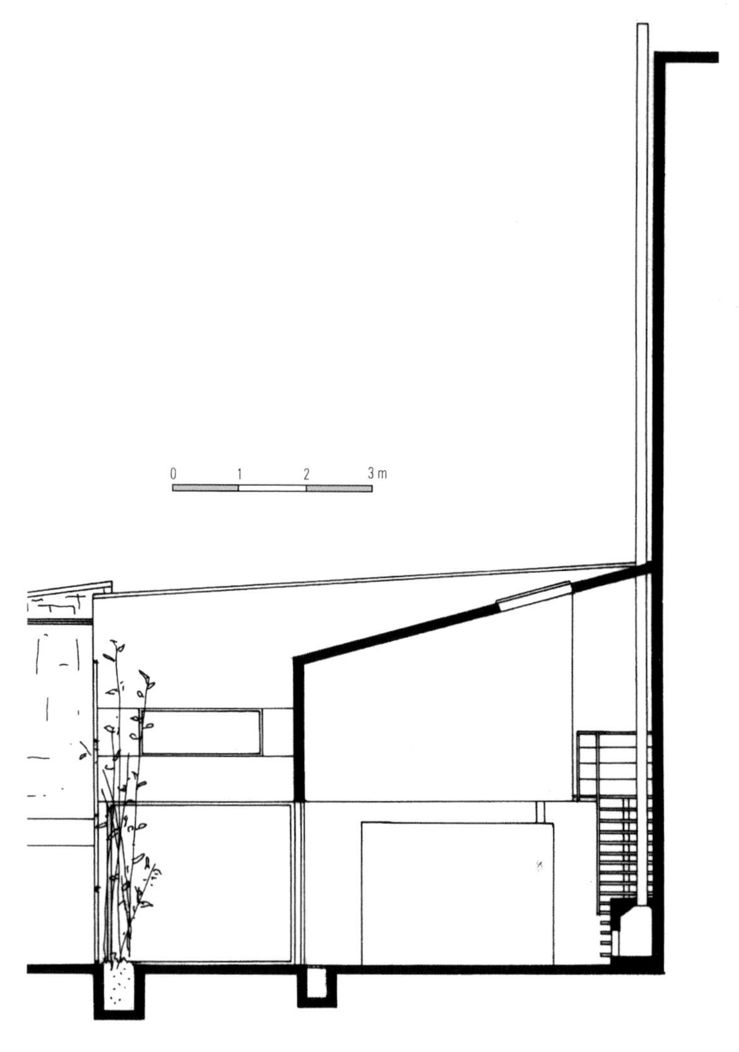

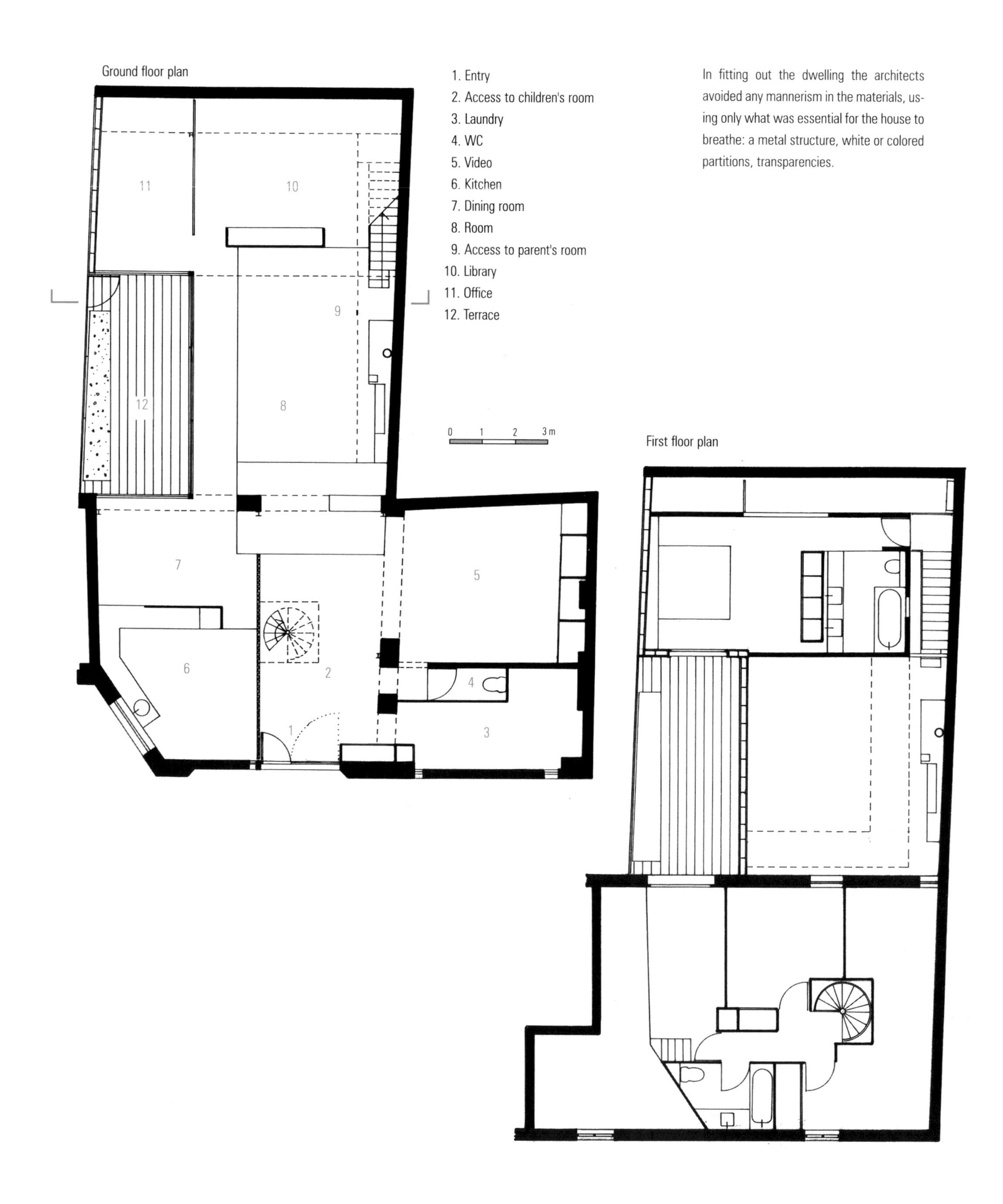

In fitting out the dwelling the architects avoided any mannerism in the materials, using only what was essential for the house to breathe: a metal structure, white or colored partitions, transparencies.

SMEG

Rather than a plot locked amid many buildings, this new place of life breathes vitality soaked in omnipresent natural lighting.

Construction detail

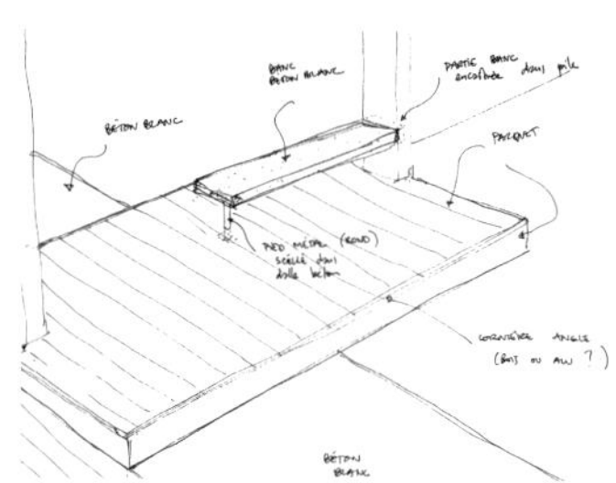

NAYA Architects (Manabu+Arata)

House in Futakoshinchi

Kawasaki-city, Kanagawa, Japan

The defining characteristic of this site is its "flagpole" shape, a narrow 15 m strip leading to a wider, irregular shape. This shape, together with the limited natural light and the densely populated surroundings created special challenges for the architects.

The design was approached from the interior. In order to create maximum space, a wall was built up to isolate the interior from a neighboring site. The inside of the house is organized with four different levels, as openly as possible.

The long, narrow approach leads to a porch and through to the entrance level. A short staircase leads to space one, and a gentle slope leads to space two. There is no clear distinction between the first and second floors, or between the living and the working areas. The spaces are all loosely connected in plan and section, without traditional rooms. Each space has a window and storage, which is created using the 4.5 mm steel plate and installed in the building frame using the sash method. Timber was used for the walls, roof and floor.

Photographs: Koui Yaginuma

The "flagpole" shape of the site, increasingly common in crowded Japanese cities, presented special challenges for the architects. The pole part of the site is 15 meters long, and the flag part is irregularly shaped.

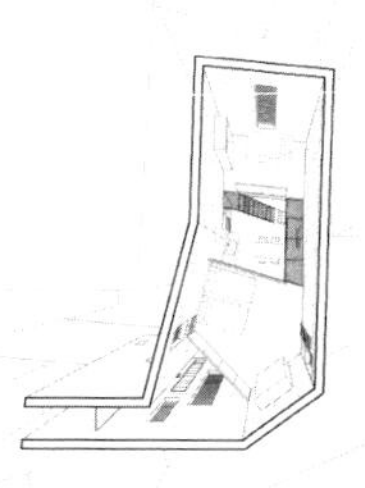

Site plan

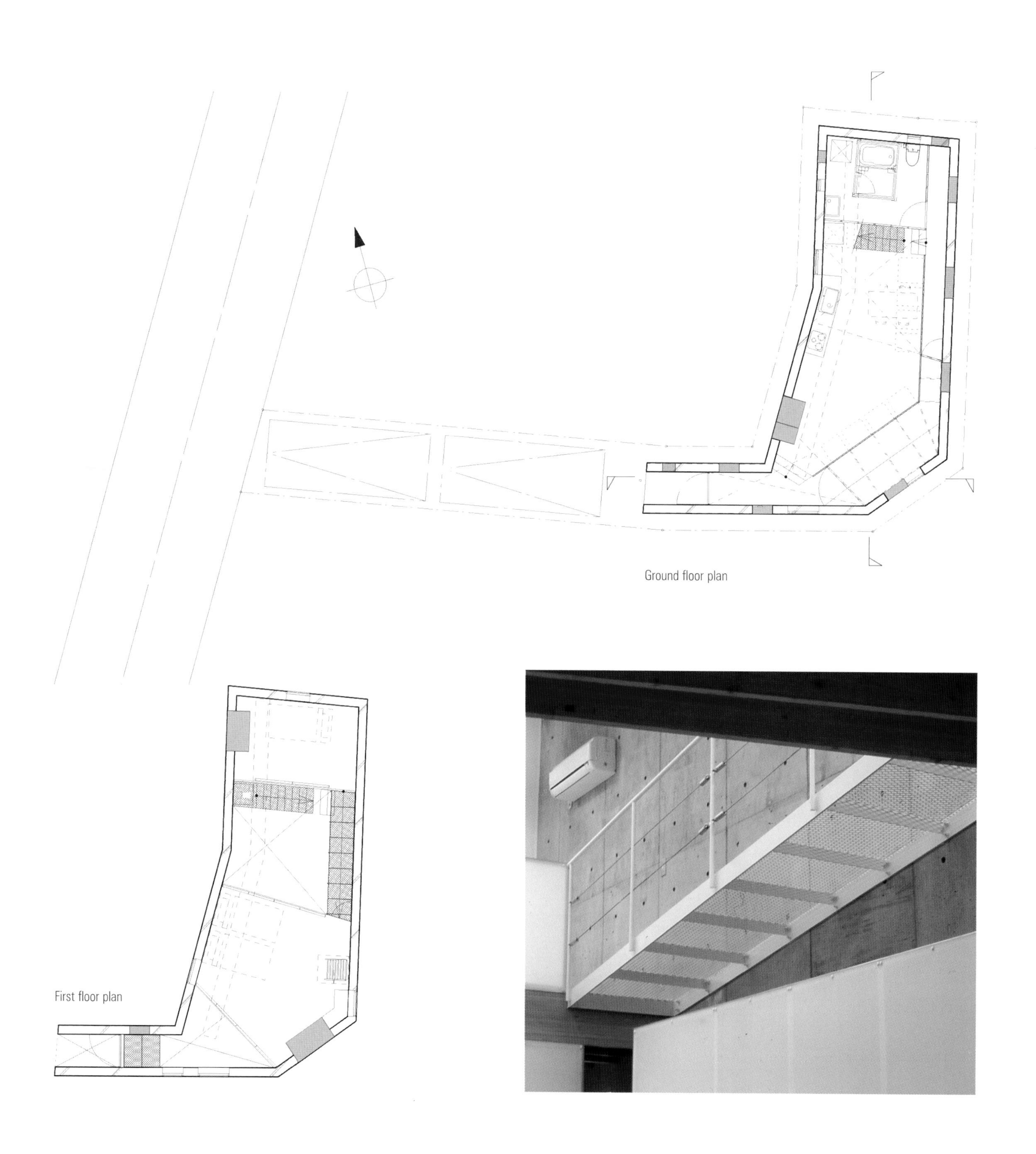
Ground floor plan
First floor plan

To create maximum interior space, the house is arranged in an open layout over four different levels, connected through staircases and ramps. A cantilever structure rises from the ground, crating a floating wooden platform.

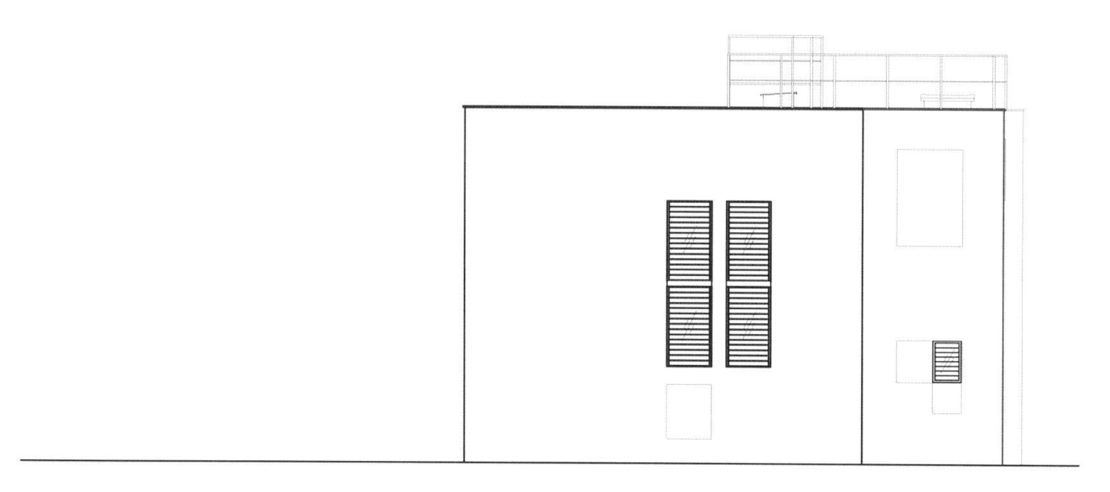

South elevation

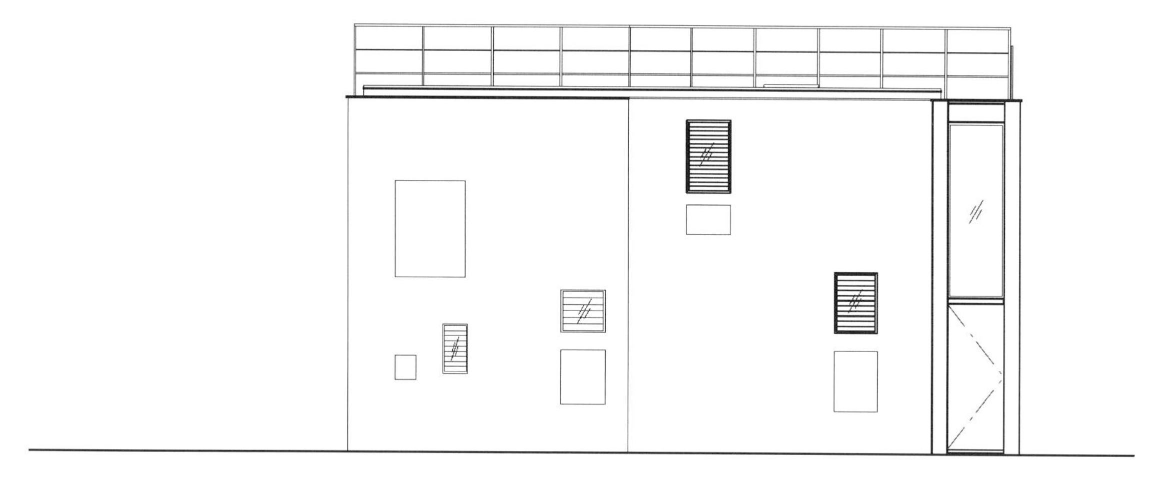

West elevation

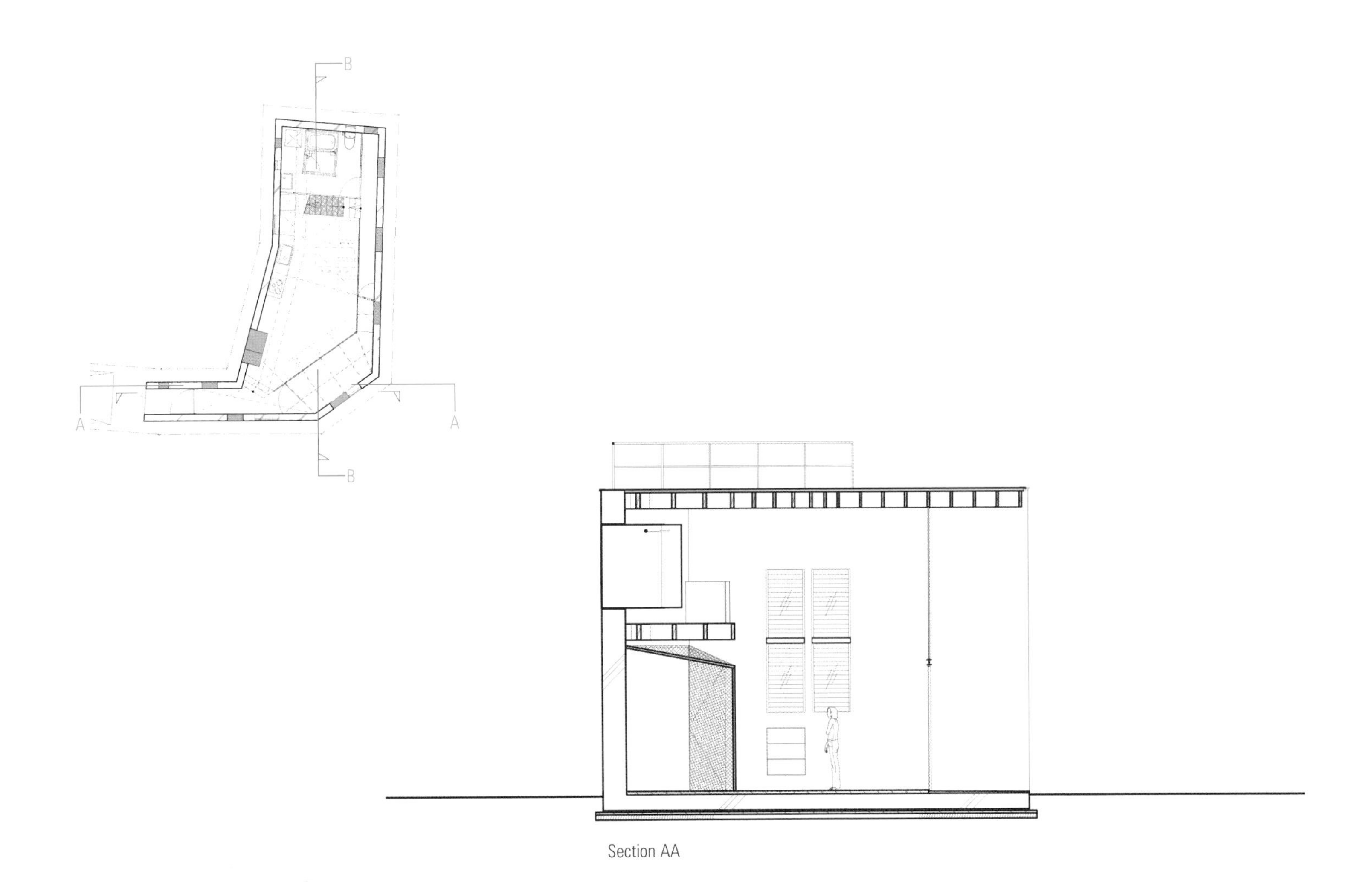

Section AA

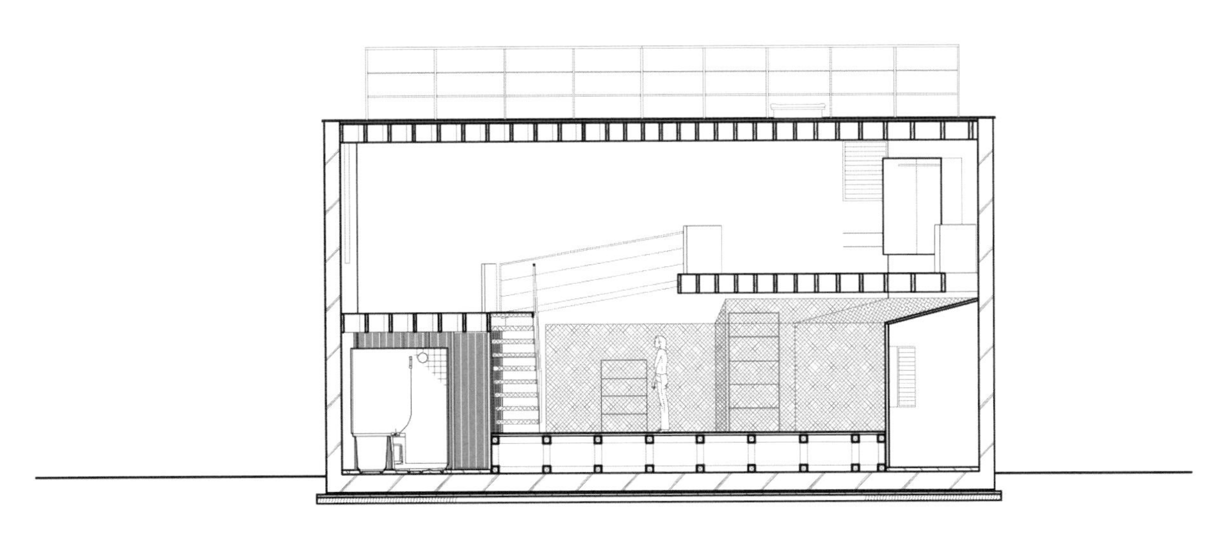

Section BB

pool Architektur

In spe-single family house

Wien, Austria

The site is determined on the one hand by a slope falling gently towards the north, and on the other by two statutory regulations restricting the possible building location: it had to be adjoined to the neighboring house and was not allowed to be more than a few meters away from the street on the southern side.
One approaches the house by gentle concrete steps gradually entrenching themselves into the ground, thus leading to the sunken entrance area situated between ground and basement floor. Along with the access steps a car ramp, which, among other things, can also be used as a covered parking space or to play table tennis, runs down to the basement level.
The kitchen/dining area, open completely to the south, is a few steps above entrance level. From this three-meter-high space, four steps lead up to the somewhat lower-height living area, expanding into the garden on the north side. A sliding door provides access to a terrace, beyond which lie a swimming pool and garden.
Turning around again, the slope of the entrance hill leads to a working area situated on top of it, between ground and first floor. Here, sunlight shines into the ground floor, and one has a fair view of the landscape and home.
Another turn, and after some steps one arrives at a small room which provides access to three individual rooms, a bathroom and a small terrace on the south side. From here, a steel stairway leads up to the roof, offering a marvellous view over Lainzerbach.

Photographs: Hertha Hurnaus

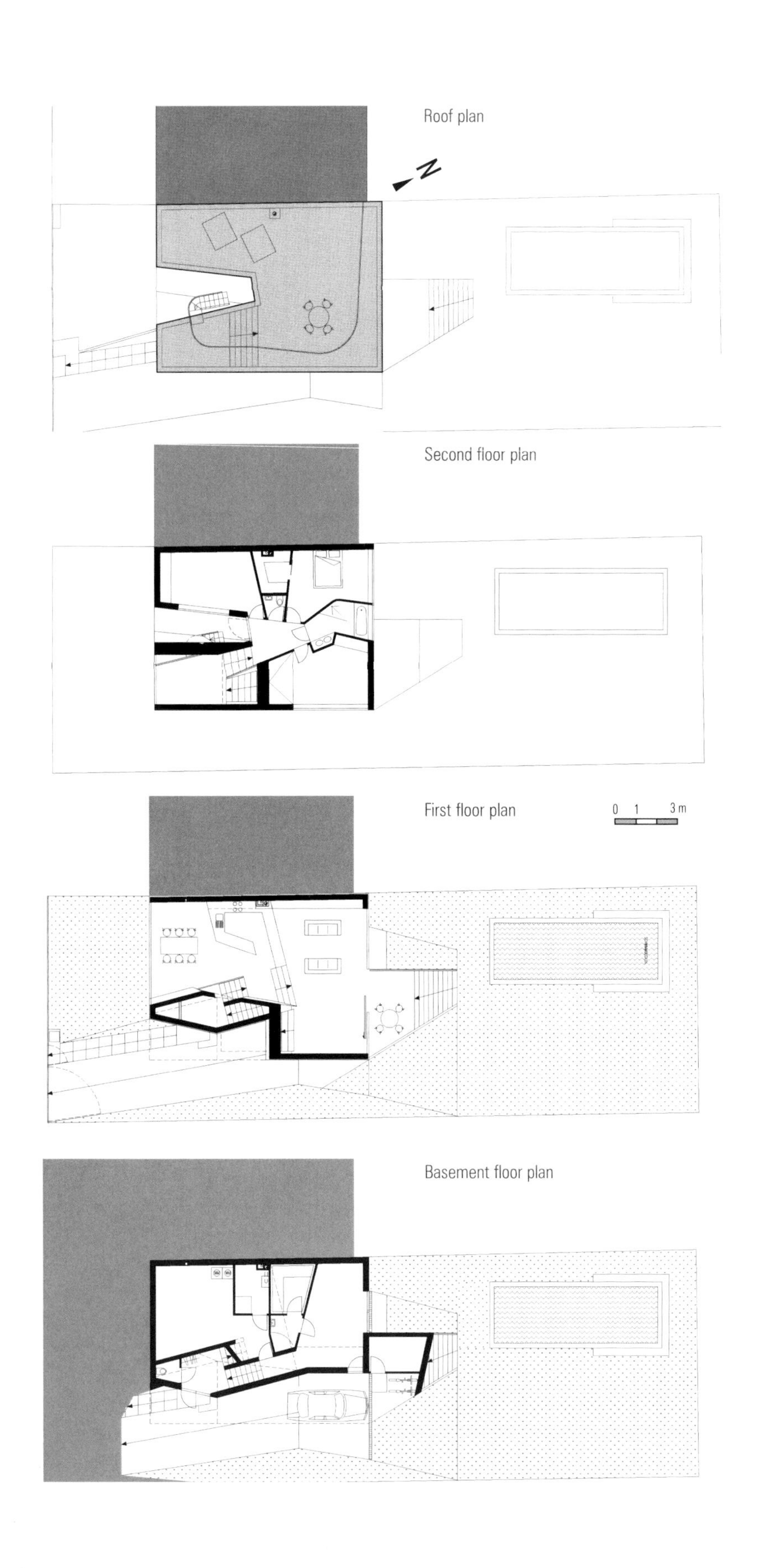
Roof plan
Second floor plan
First floor plan
0 1 3 m
Basement floor plan

POST
W 84973 F

East elevation

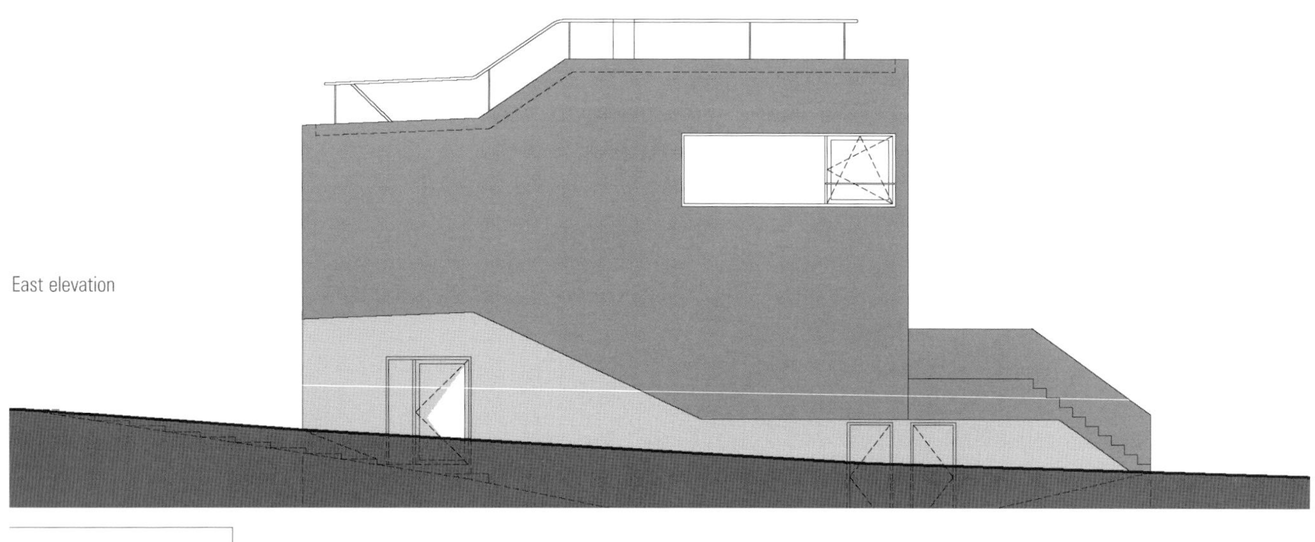

The northern and southern elevations are cut open completely, the southern glazed facade flooding the interior with light. Once inside, visitors find themselves in the inside of a cut-up hill, looking down on the one side to the basement, on the other side climbing up into the living area on the ground fllor.

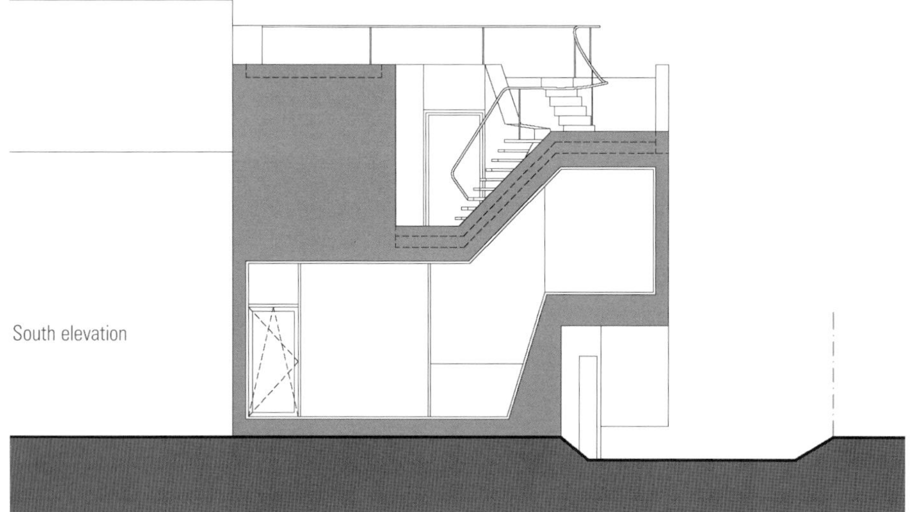

South elevation

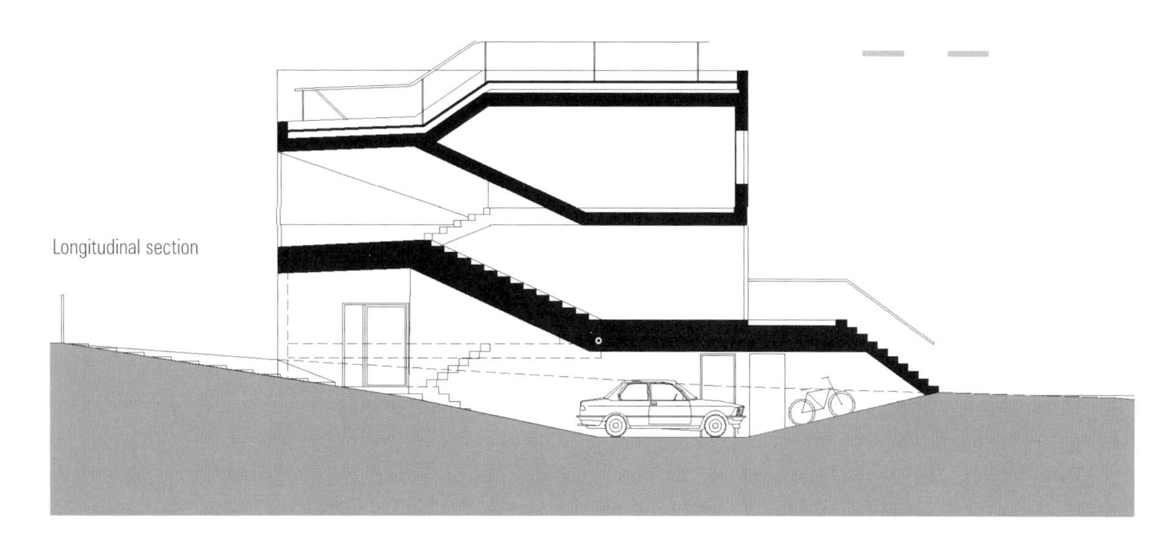

Longitudinal section

Claesson Koivisto Rune

No.5 House

Nacka, Sweden

The starting point for this house for a graphic designer and his family (the client designed the No. 5 sign himself) was a simple structure where the inside would be as important as the outside. The design was developed as a geometric volume, a kind of inverted volume that can be read either as a box with a series of openings, or an open space with a series of closures.
The construction method involved establishing a grid based on standard dimensions for building materials, and then superimposing it onto the basic box structure. This grid was used to create the basic room structure for the house, which included three bedrooms, a bathroom and one larger living/dining space with kitchen. One of the four sides of each of the main rooms was completely glazed, allowing natural light into the house and blurring the distinction between interior and exterior. The bedrooms and living area are basically open towards one cardinal point each, meaning there is an opening in each facade. Even though the bedrooms are quite small, the surrounding landscape becomes part of the space, creating a sense of vastness. The bathroom, which has no wall opening, has a roof window instead. A glazed doorway leading out from the living area to a partially walled terrace creates an outdoor room that is open to the sky at one end and open to the view at the other.

Photographs: Åke E:son Lindman

A homogenous steel framework was used to transfer the load evenly over the entire roof surface. The major loads of the roof construction are supported by gables, while the staggered and sloping levels of the rooftop landscape serve to achieve a spatial flow largely unhampered by supports. The interior space is designed as a loft whose various functional areas are defined by different floor levels.

Site plan

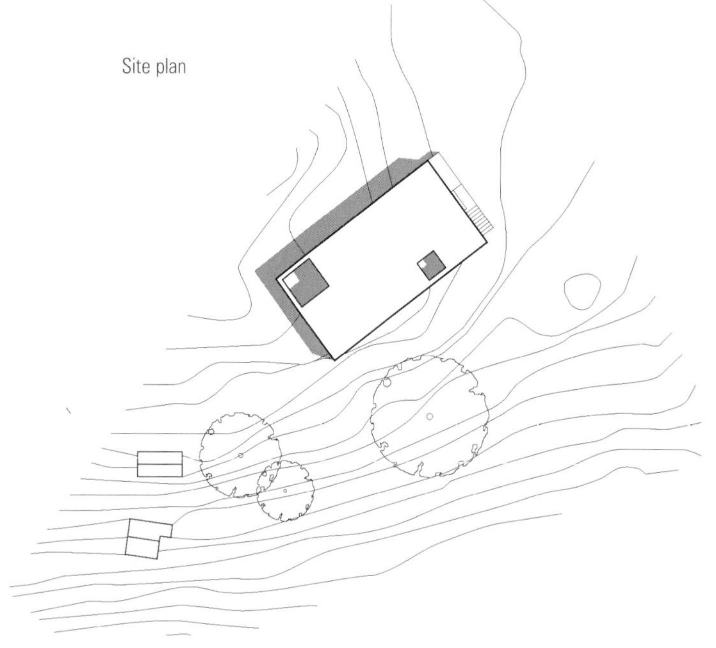

Northeast elevation
Southeast elevation
Southwest elevation
Northwest elevation

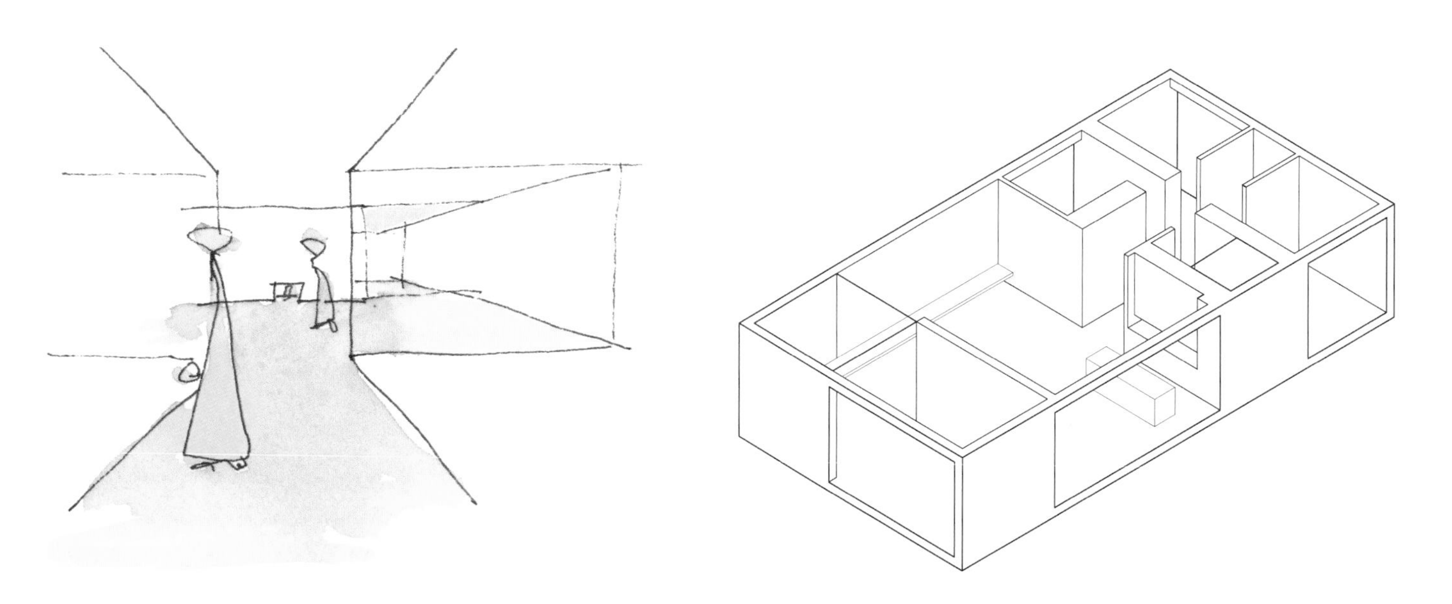

5

1. Entrance
2. Bedroom
3. Master bedroom
4. Kitchen
5. Living
6. Terrace

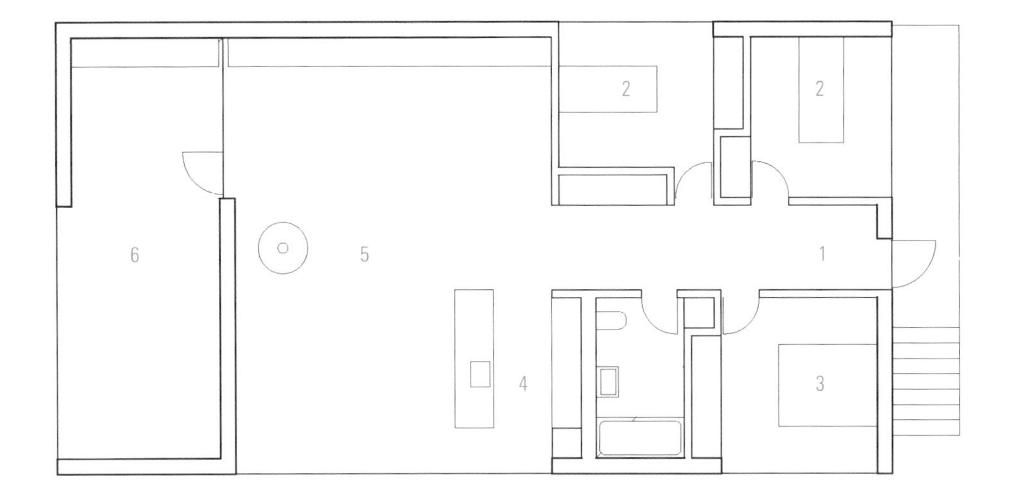

earning to Fly
Set the Control fo
Echoes

Esteve Terradas

House in Gaüses

Gaüses, Spain

The house is located on a 500 m² rectangular site, in an area where planning laws allow the use of the entire width of the site, but restrict new buildings to a single story.

To create a small house that would be as open as possible, the architect used the concept of a large verandah (a house-verandah), so that the facades would be conceived as sliding doors that could be fully opened in order to blur the distinction between the indoor space and the garden.

The roof plays an important role, helping to achieve transparency and create the similarity to a large verandah. The facades were built using Tecnal aluminum joinery that resembles steel.

The design is simple and consists of three different areas. The first is the main bedroom, dressing room and main bathroom, next to a reading area and study. The central area is the sitting room and entry, while the third area contains a kitchen-dining room and a small bedroom with its own bathroom. A large red sliding door allows this area to be separated from the rest.

In total, the building covers 98 m², while the rest of the site is used as a garden.

The house is closed off with blinds along its 14 meter main facade, around 3 m from the sliding aluminum doors, leaving a space that can be used to extend the house.

Photographs: Jordi Canosa

Floor plan
1. Living room
2. Kitchen-Dining room
3. Bedroom
4. Bathroom
5. Bedroom-Studio
6. Closet

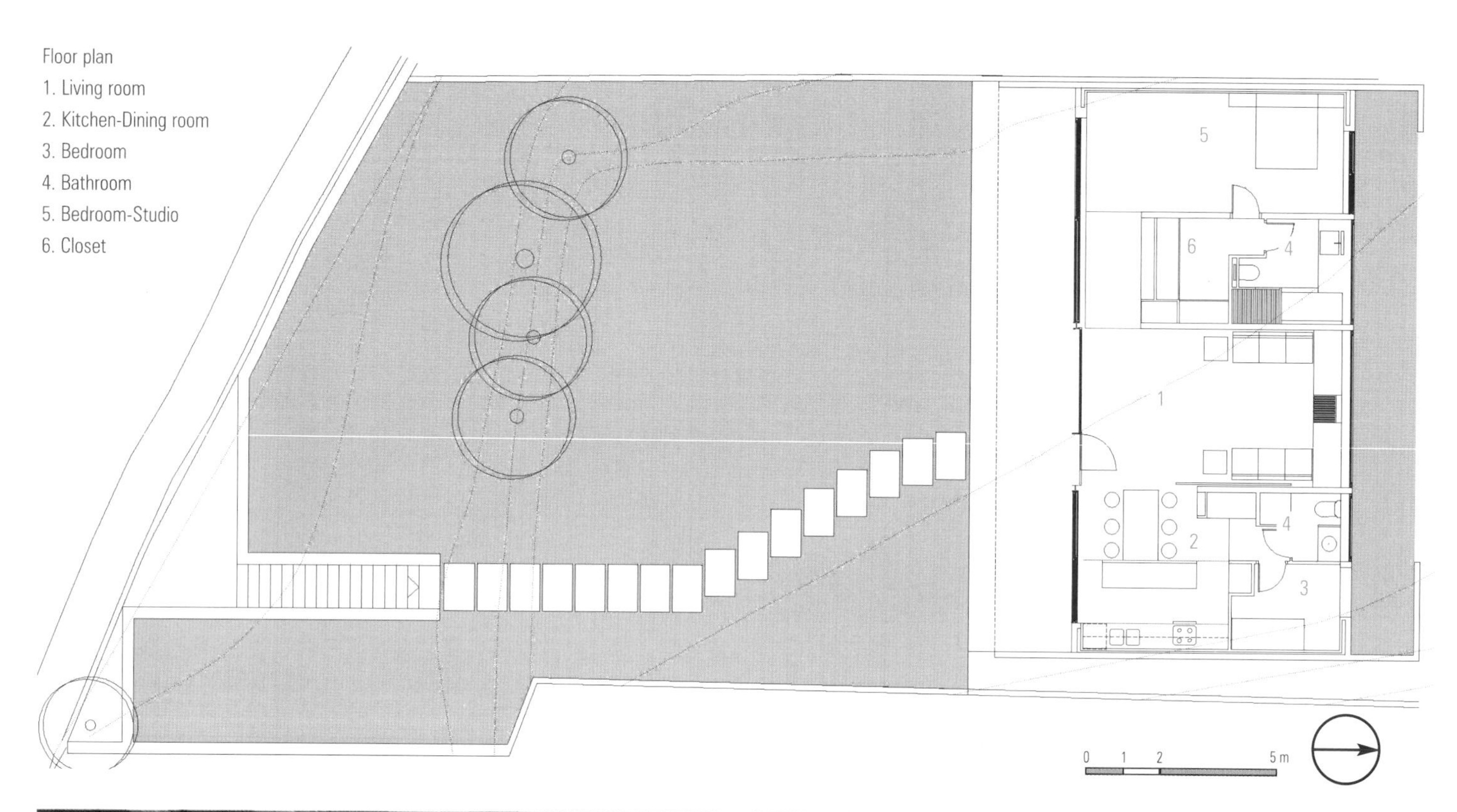

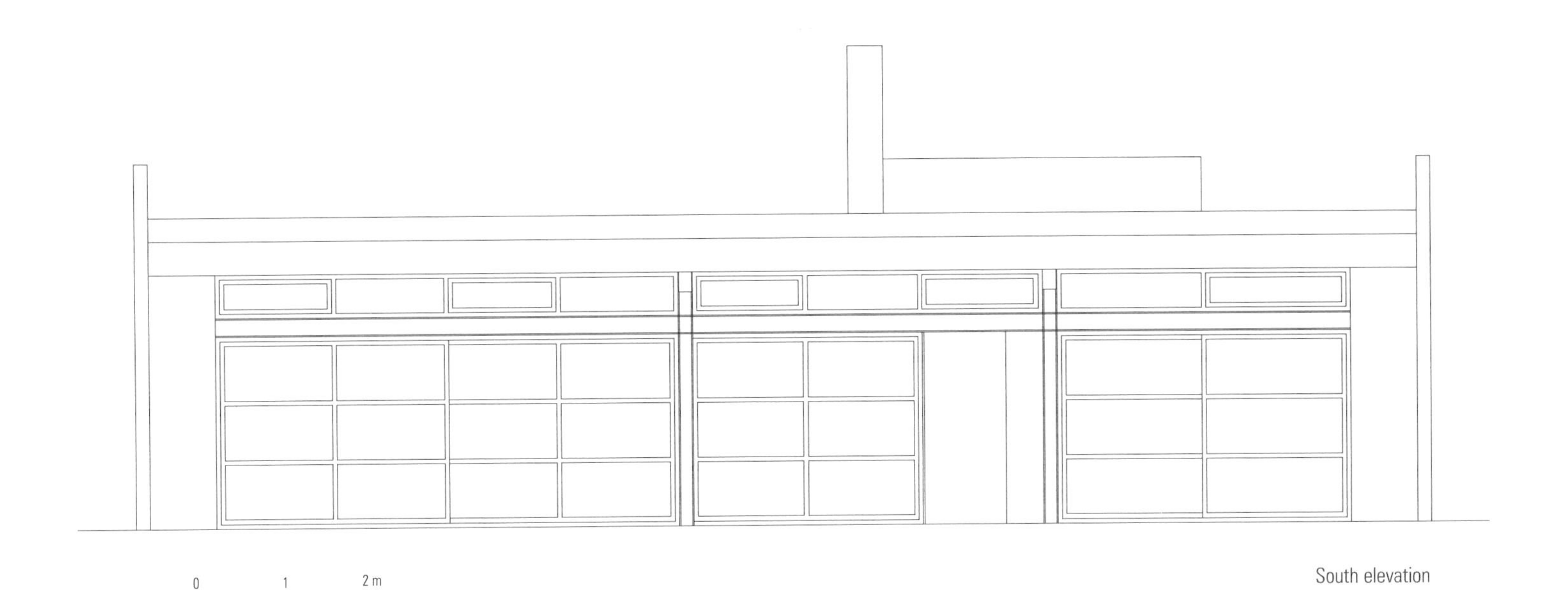

South elevation

Cross section

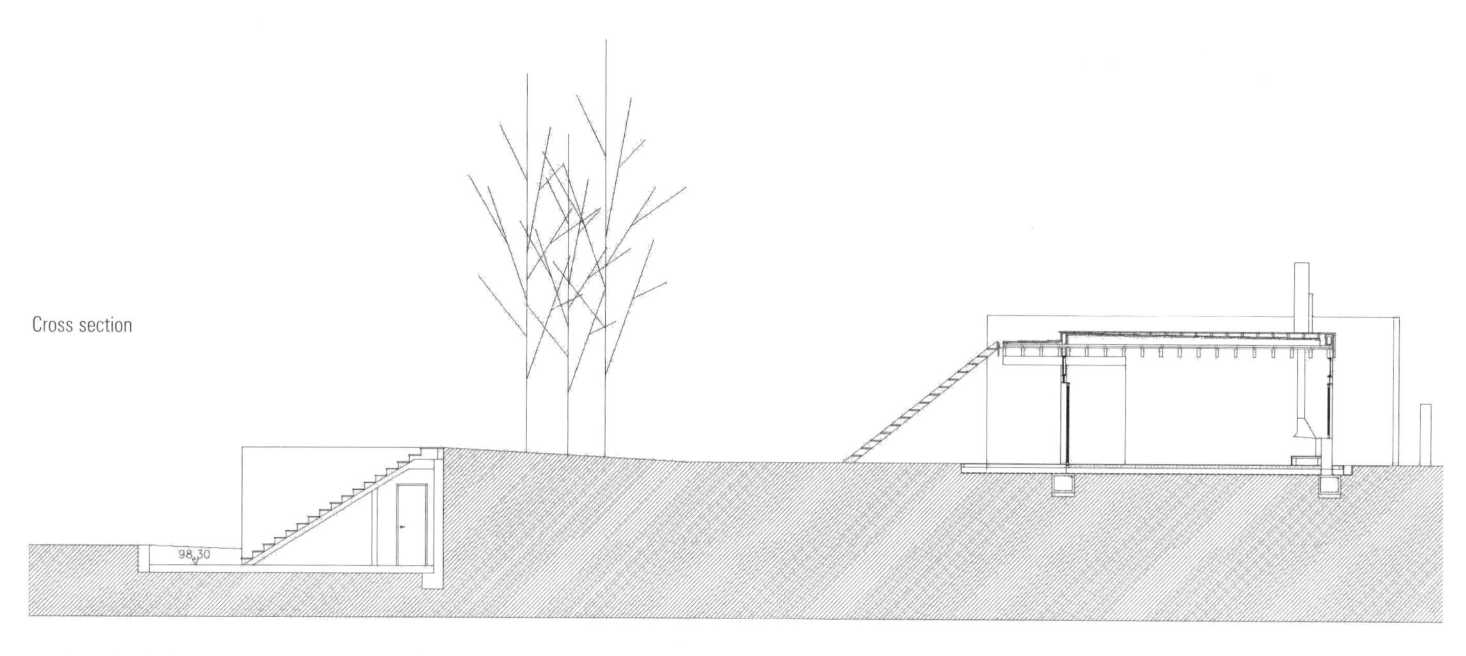

The house is built on a 14 x 7 m rectangular base, with a surface plan measuring 98 m2. The rest of the 500 m2 site is devoted to a large garden.
Along the main facade, the house is closed of by large blinds, with a 3 meter space between the doors and the blinds that can alternate as interior and exterior space.

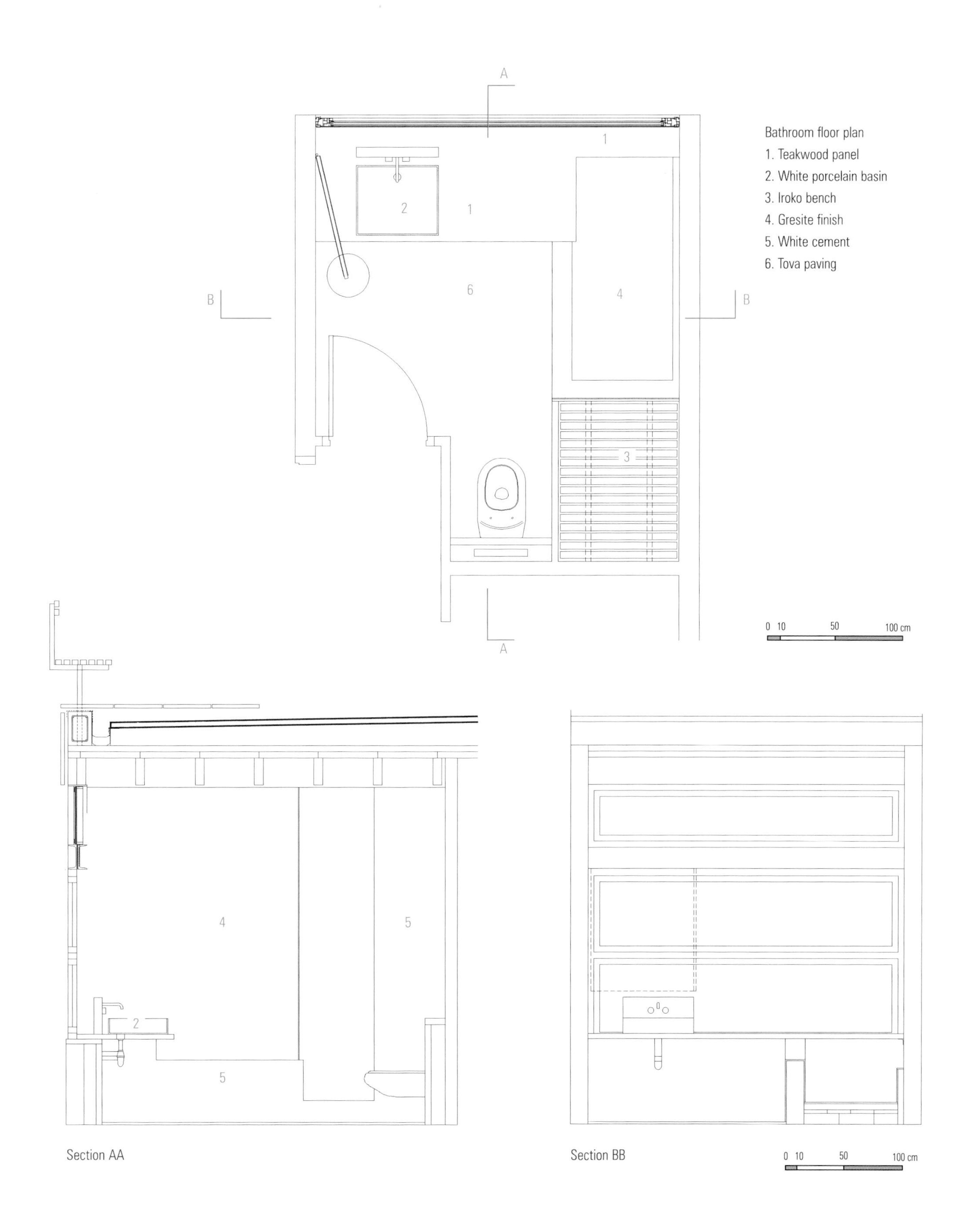

Bathroom floor plan

1. Teakwood panel
2. White porcelain basin
3. Iroko bench
4. Gresite finish
5. White cement
6. Tova paving

Section AA

Section BB

FOBA / Katsu Umebayashi

Aura House

Tokyo, Japan

In the amorphous complexity of central Tokyo, urban structure occurs at scales imperceptible to the pedestrian observer. Forms are either incoherent or irrelevant; the urban experience is a succession of interior spaces.
Here, a house requires few facilities. To eat, you go to a restaurant; to bathe, you go to the sento (public baths); to exercise, you go to the gym; to be entertained, you go to the cinema. The ultimate Tokyo house is somehow like an art gallery: an empty, inward-looking space, perhaps with unusual lighting.
The Aura house is located in a typical Japanese "eel's nest" site: an alley 3.5 meters wide by 21.5 meters long. The challenge was to bring light and air into the center of the house. Rather than using the traditional tsubo-niwa (courtyard garden), the architects opted instead for optimizing both the available light and the potential floor area.
Concrete walls were run down either side of the site and a translucent membrane was stretched between them. In order to sustain tension in the roof fabric, a complex curve was created by making the two walls identical but reversed. Cylindrical concrete beams brace the two walls. The opposing ridge lines cause the orientation of the beams to twist along the length of the building - despite appearances, a rational structural solution. The fabric skin filters sunlight by day, and glows by night: the building pulses, "breathing" light with the 24-hour rhythm of the city.

Photographs: Tohru Waki (Shokokusha Pub. Co.,Ltd.)

The plot is wedged into an alley 3.5 meters wide by 21.5 meters long. Rather than using the traditional *tsuboniwa* (courtyard garden), the architects opted instead for optimizing both the available light and the potential floor area.

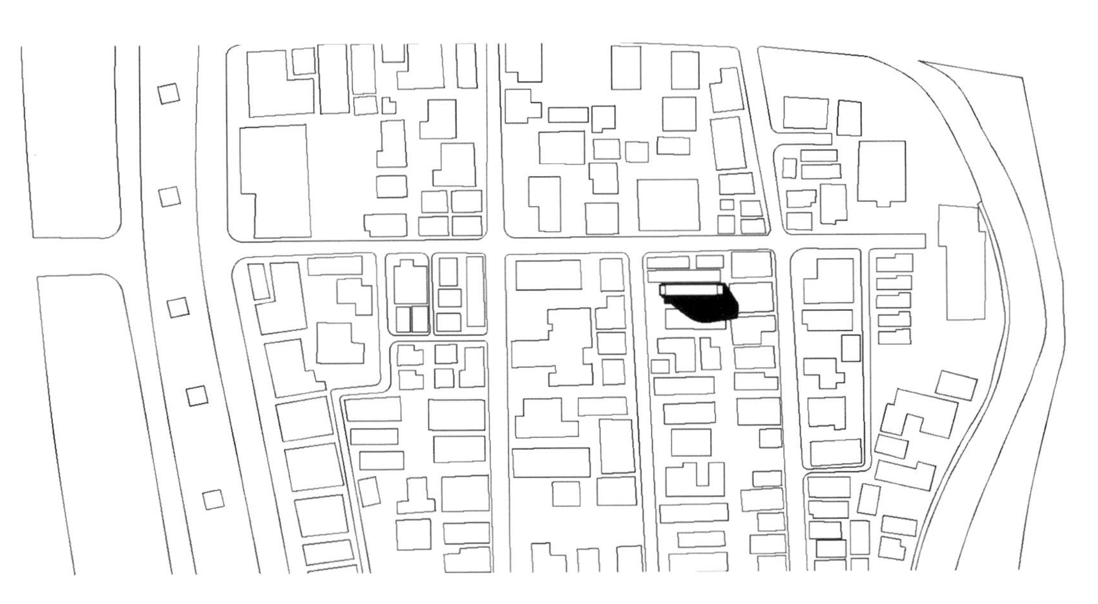

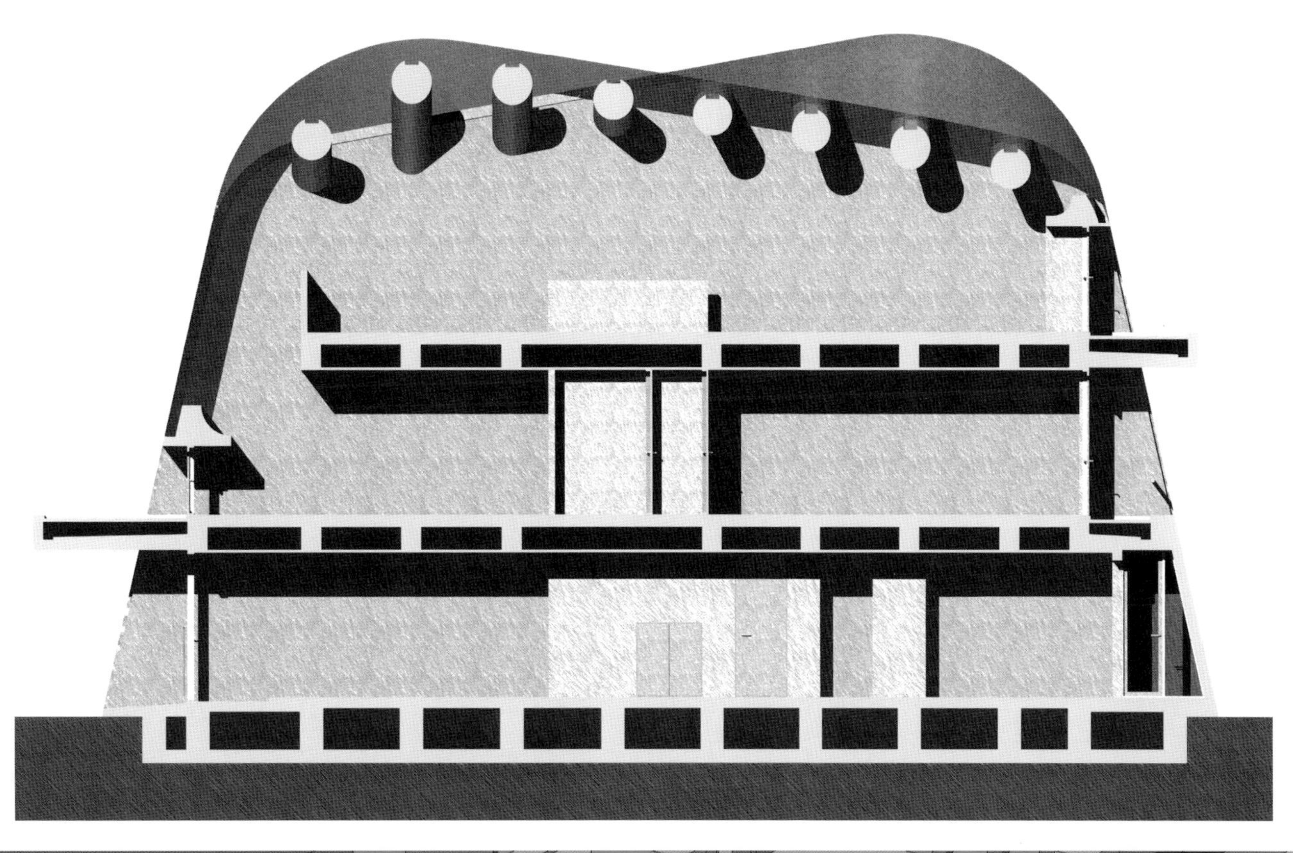

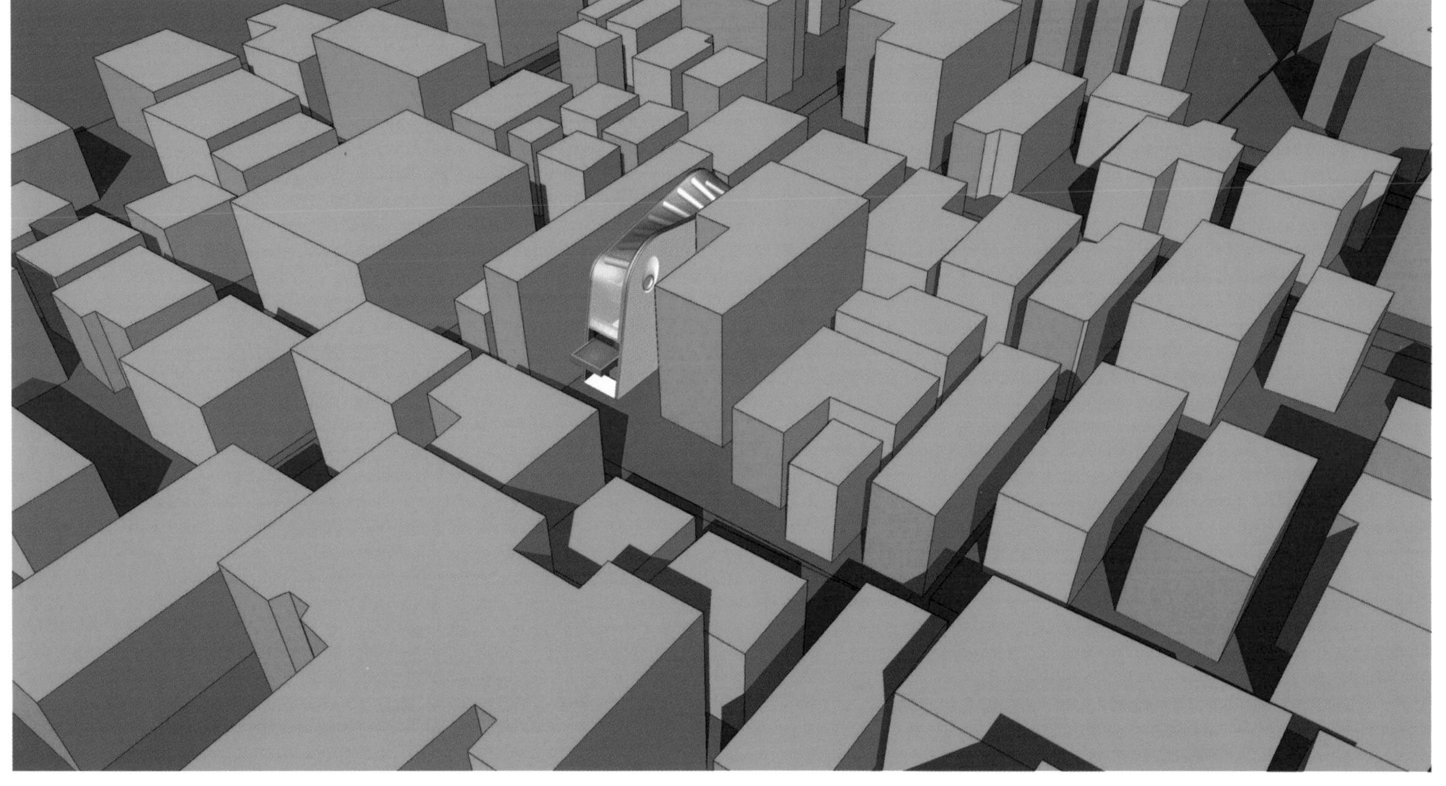

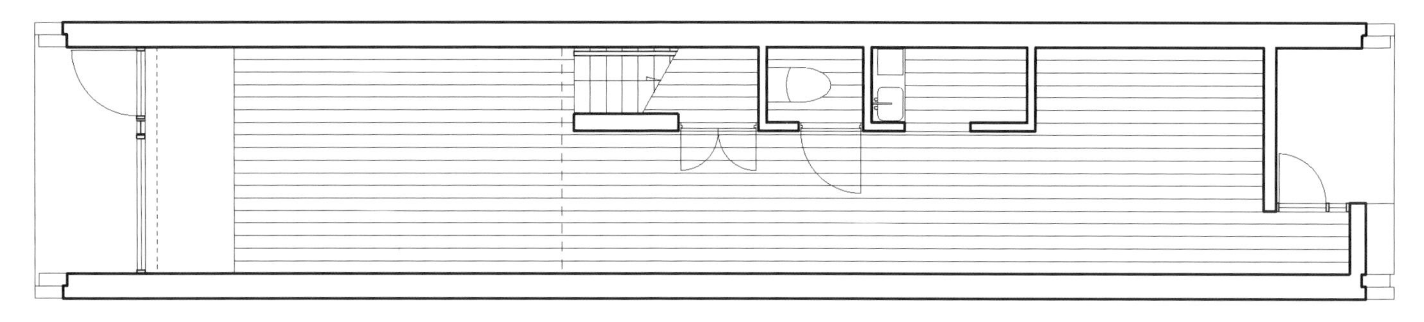

Ground floor plan

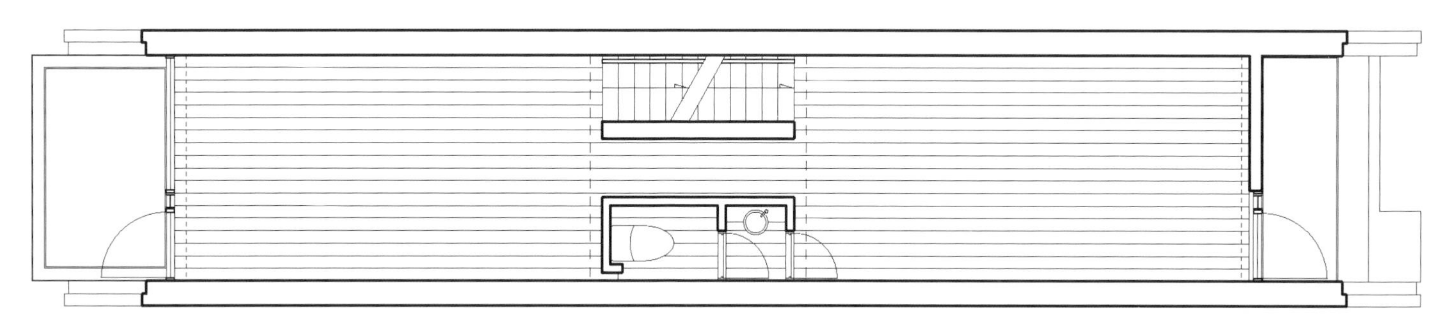

First floor plan

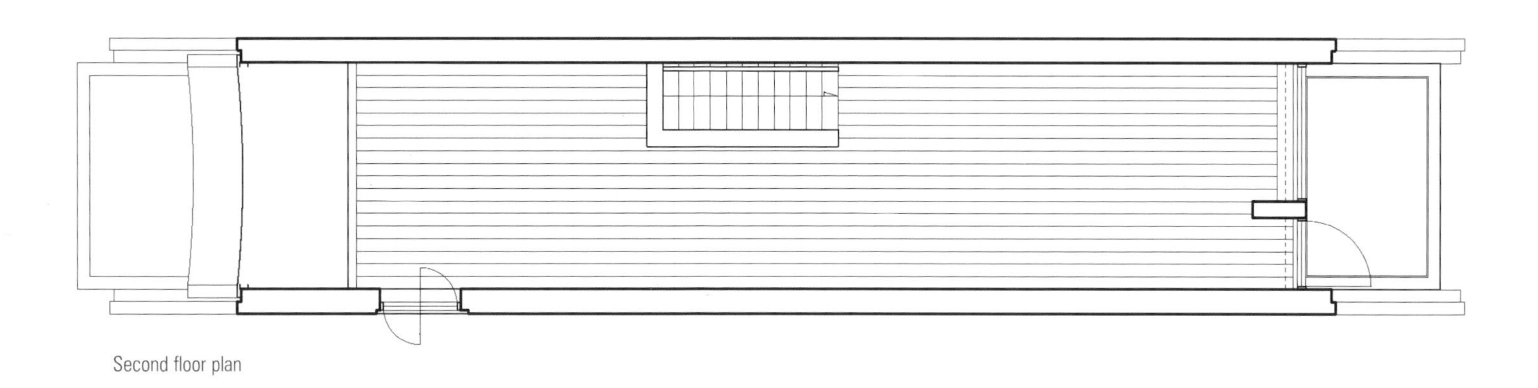

Second floor plan

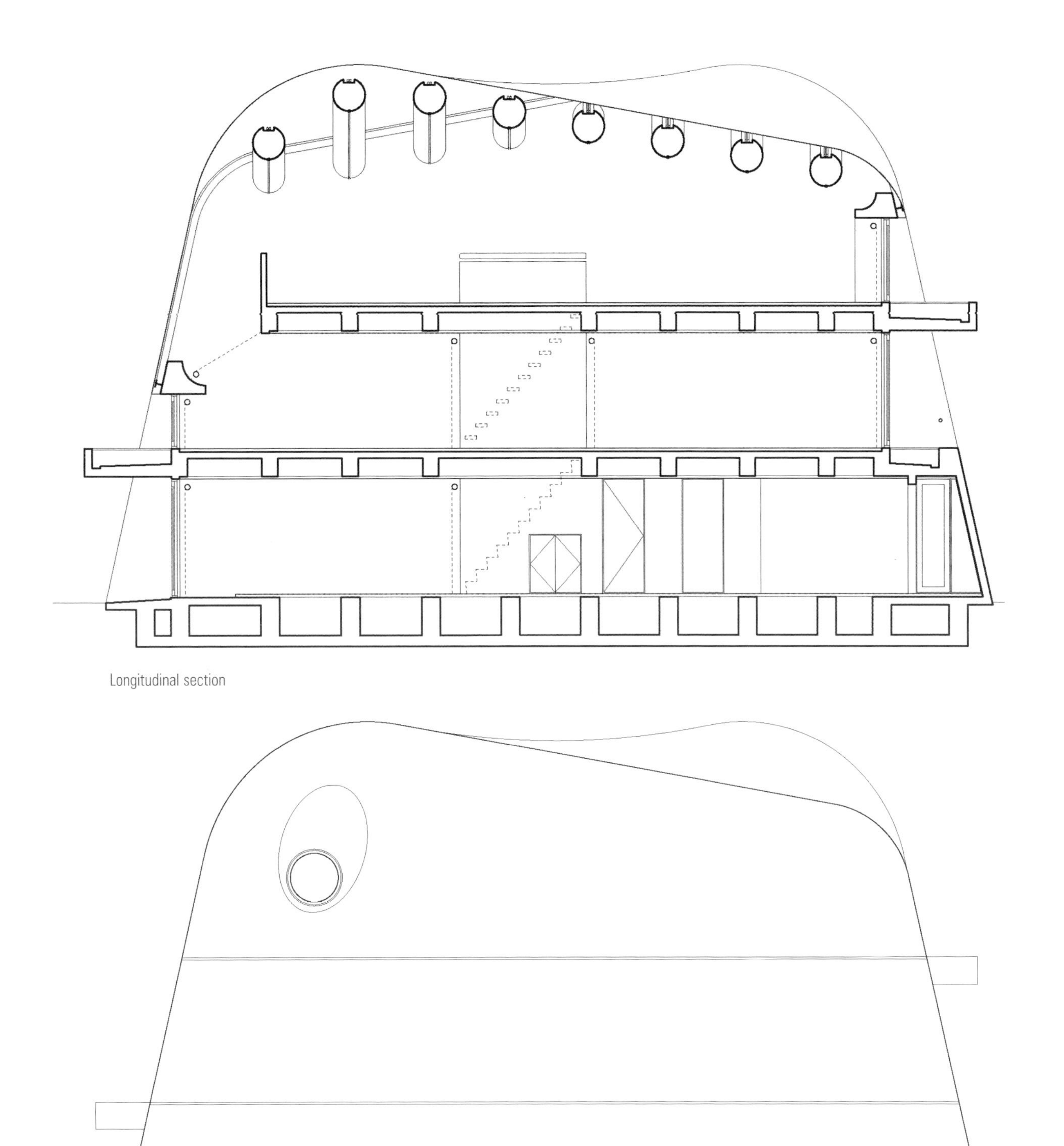

Longitudinal section

Side elevation

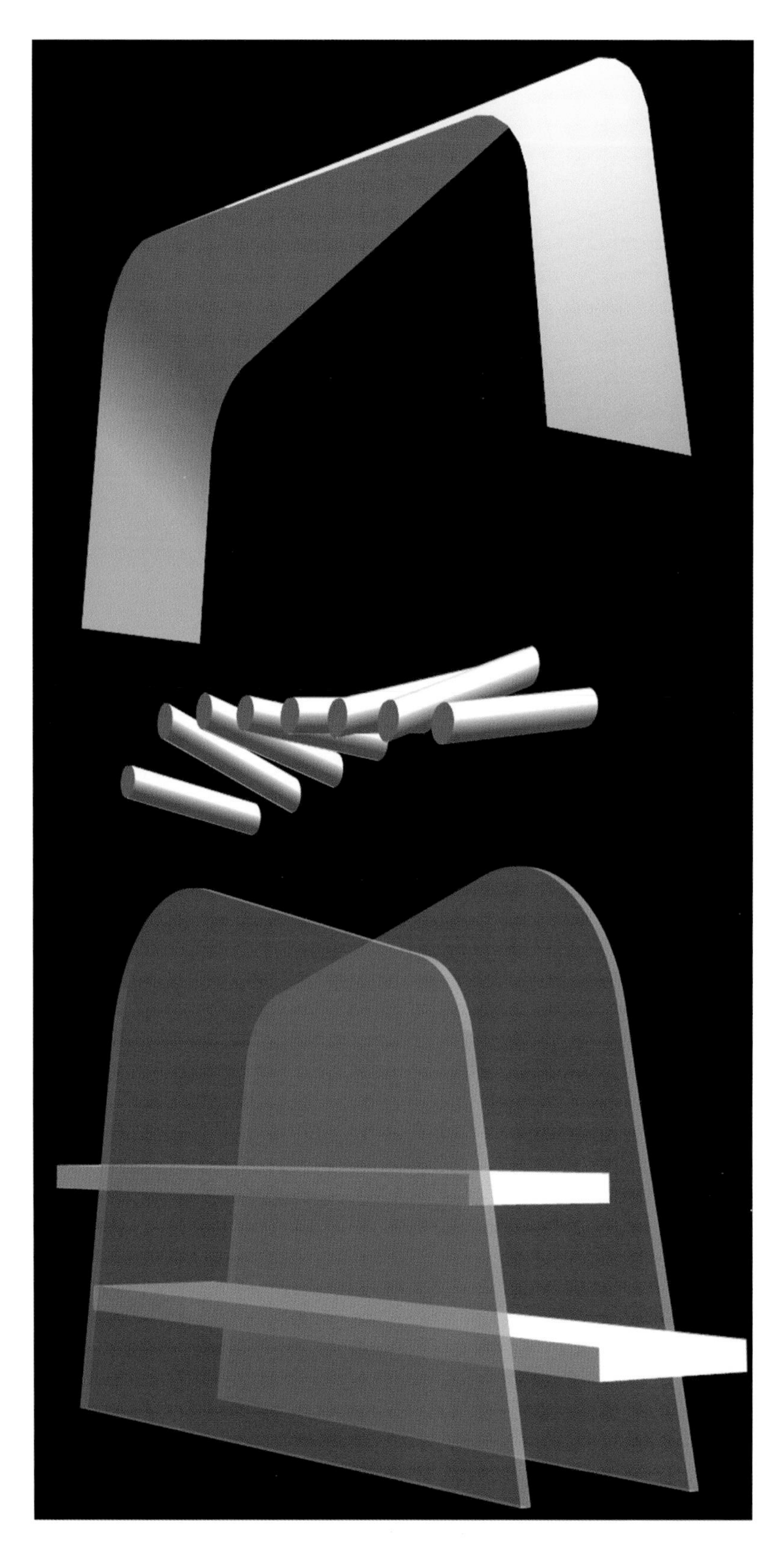

Concrete walls were run down either side of the site and a translucent membrane was stretched between them. In order to sustain tension in the roof fabric, a curve was created by making the two walls identical but reversed. Cylindrical concrete beams brace the two walls.

Construction details

Studio Aisslinger

Loftcube

Berlin, Germany

"What could a minimal home unit look like - a temporary retreat where urban nomads in big cities and dense urban zones could find privacy?" In answering his question, Aisslinger has discovered a wealth of unused real estate in big cities: the flat roofs of high-rise buildings. His Loftcube is the ideal "home away from home" for young mobile professionals. It can be transported either by dismantling it piece by piece or by relocating the entire unit by helicopter or crane. Once in place, it can be hooked up to the building's utilities connections.

This futuristic concept has been realized by employing DuPont materials Corian, Zodiaq, and Antron. Bearing in mind the growing trend toward home offices, Aisslinger has designed two Loftcubes - a "home" and an "office" version, each of which covers 36 m^2.

The "home" version is segmented into living and sleeping areas, kitchen and bathroom. To divide the space, special Corian partitioning panels with an unusual double function were developed. For example, the wall panel between the kitchen and bathroom features an integrated water tap that can be manoeuvred to both sides, and used both in the kitchen sink and the washbasin. The showerhead in the functional panel that separates the living area from the bathroom works along the same lines - the faucet can be moved either to the shower on one side and the plant pots on the other.

The body can be customized according to the user's desires. The four outer walls consist of individual segments, which are available in transparent, translucent or closed versions. Louvre windows with horizontal wooden lamellae provide ventilation, while fixed and sliding panels provide individual partitioning of the interior space.

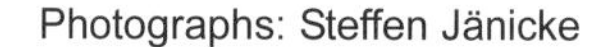
Photographs: Steffen Jänicke

The body of the cube sits 1.2 meters from the ground and has a total height of three meters. The four outer walls, each measuring 6.6 meters in length, consist of individual segments, which are available in transparent, translucent or closed versions. Louvre windows with horizontal wooden lamellae provide ventilation, while fixed and sliding panels provide individual partitioning of the interior space.

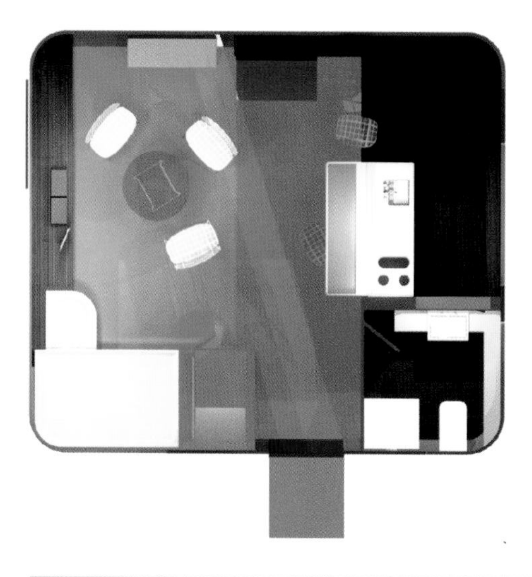

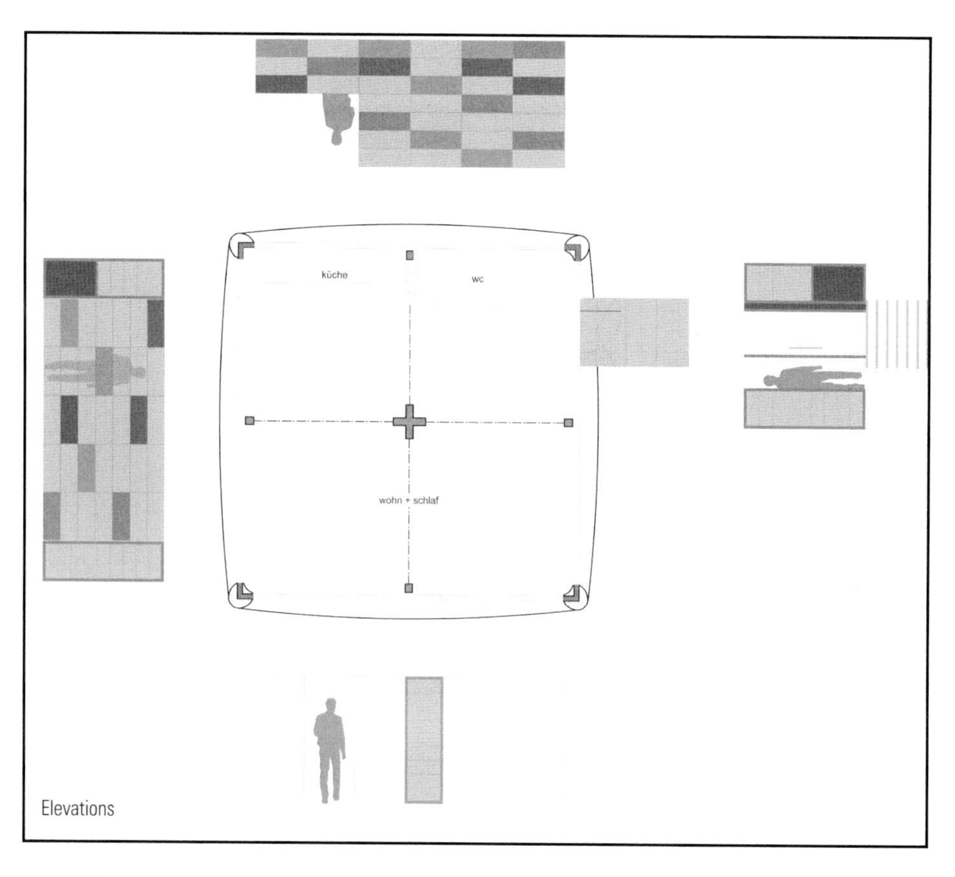

Elevations

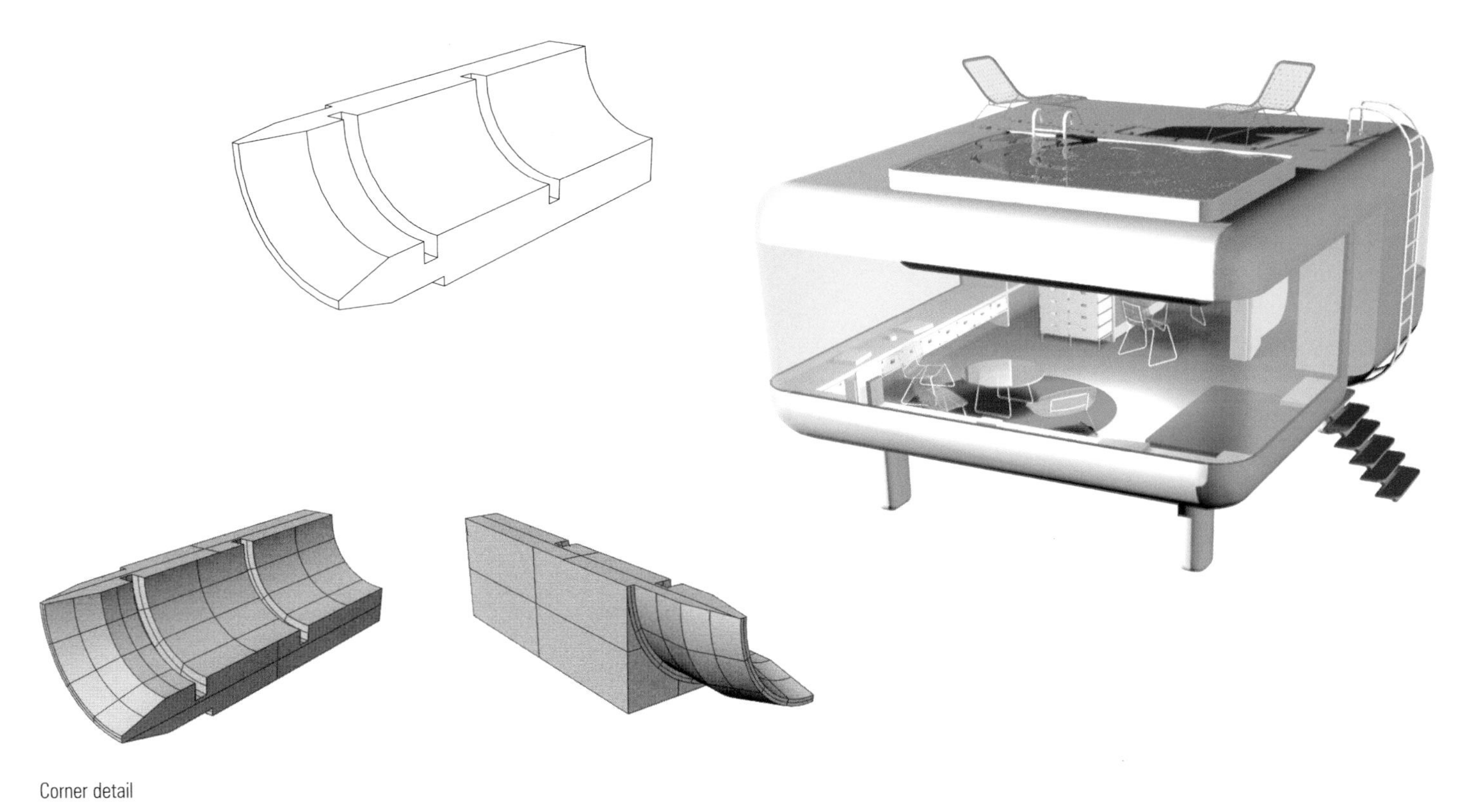

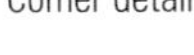

Corner detail

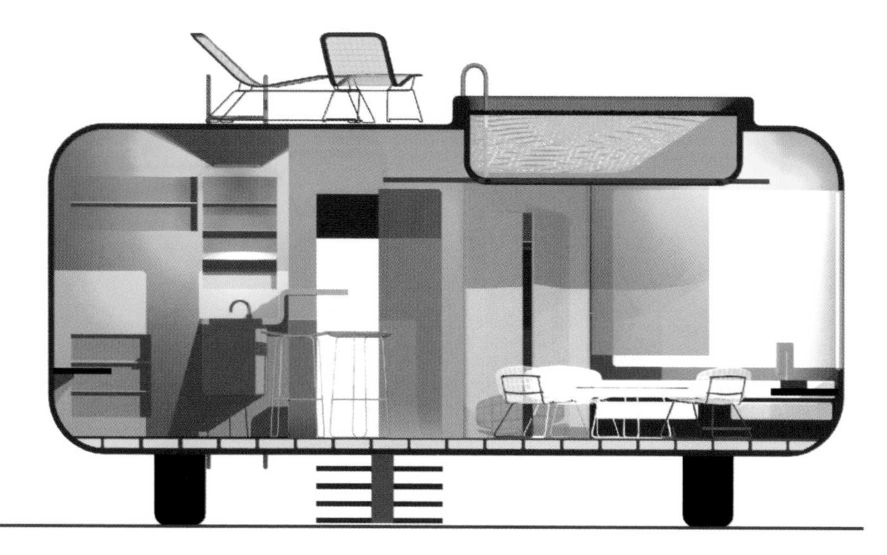

Given such limited space, specialized partitioning panels with dual functions were developed. For example, the Corian panel separating the living area from the bathroom features a faucet that can be used for the shower on one side and to water plants on the other.

Corian, a meterial whose seamlessness, thermoformability and durability made it the ideal choice for the kitchen, was used to create the shaped kitchen unit. The material chosen for the kitchen floor was Zodiaq (by DuPont), a surface material made almost entirely of quartz crystals.

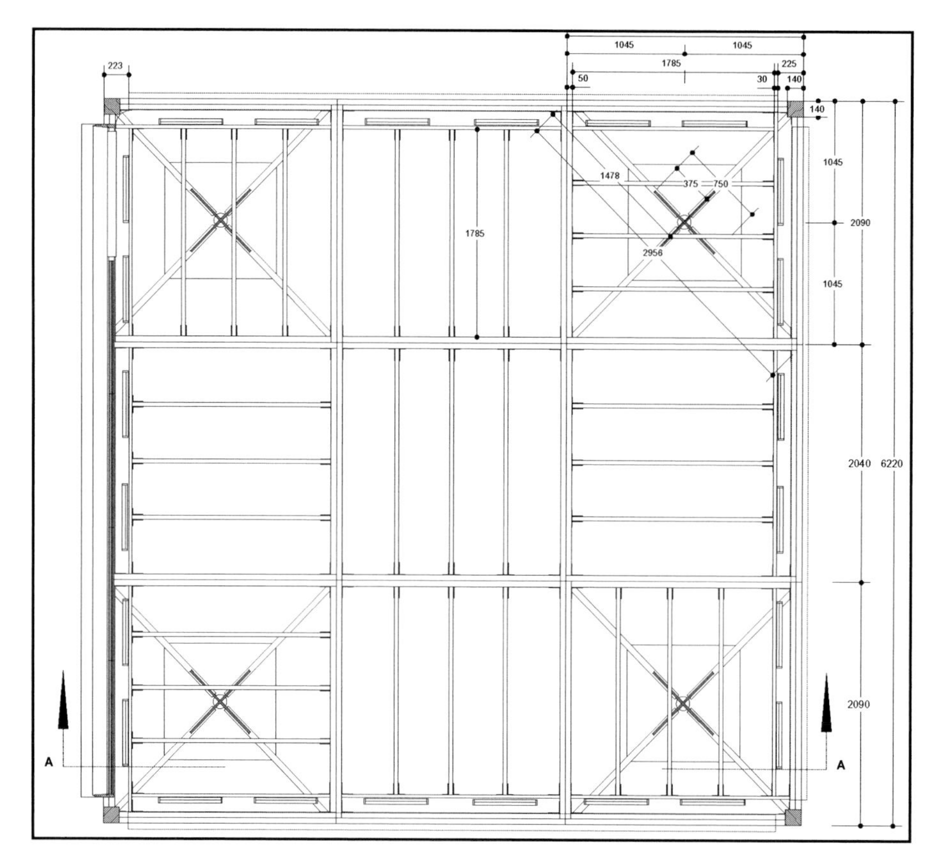

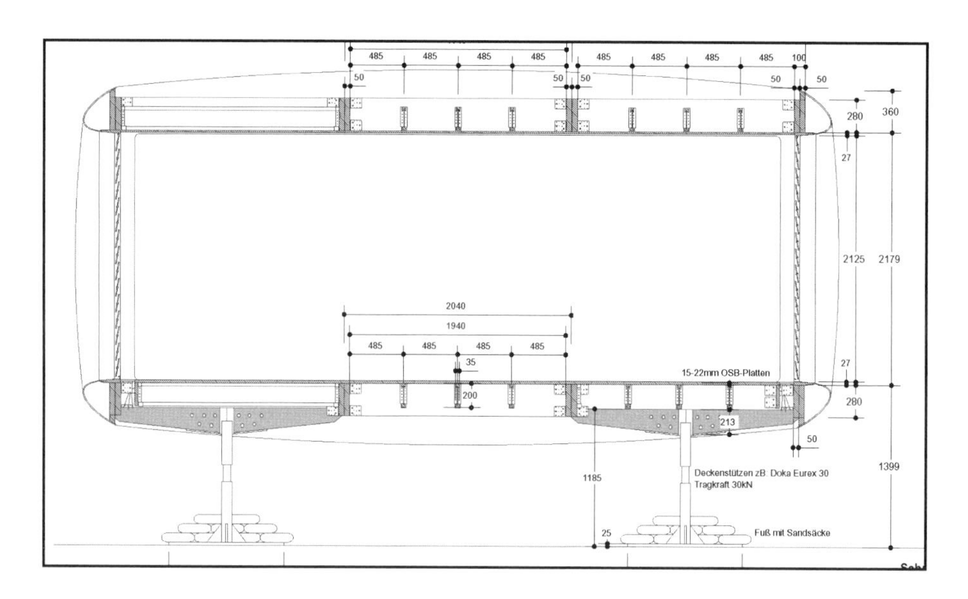
15-22mm OSB-Platten
Deckenstützen zB. Doka Eurex 30
Tragkraft 30kN
Fuß mit Sandsäcke

Moriko Kira

Weekend House Hakone

Tokyo, Japan

Weekend House Hakone is a small wooden house in a holiday village approximately 120 km southwest of Tokyo. The requirement to create a simple, tranquil house was complicated by the characteristics of the site. The challenge was to create the feeling of a house in a forest on a site located in a woody mountainous area but quite near to other housing and facing a road to the south.

The architects chose to apply a simple saddleback roof structure, which means that the ceiling height changes according to the depth of the space. By stretching the space north- and southwards, they created areas of varying heights, views and light within a single open space. This allowed them to manipulate the characteristics of space according to the conditions of light, view and privacy.

The living room, which stretches from the top of the roof towards the south, is the most intimate space with quite a low ceiling. Near the top, along the balcony, there is an area with sliding doors that allow a view of the sunny forest into the house. Because the kitchen and the bathroom stretch further towards the mountain, they visually close off the view of the neighboring lots from the balcony. Hence, inside it feels as if the house is standing alone in nature.

On the outside the house appears like a dark shape, an isolated object fading into the forest. The west and east façades are made of western red cedar colored with charcoal, while the north and south façades are covered with galvanized steel which extends the roof. In contrast, the interior is very light and has been designed to capture all the available natural light. The walls are white stucco and the floor is cedar colored in light gray.

Photographs: Satoshi Asakawa / ZOOM inc.

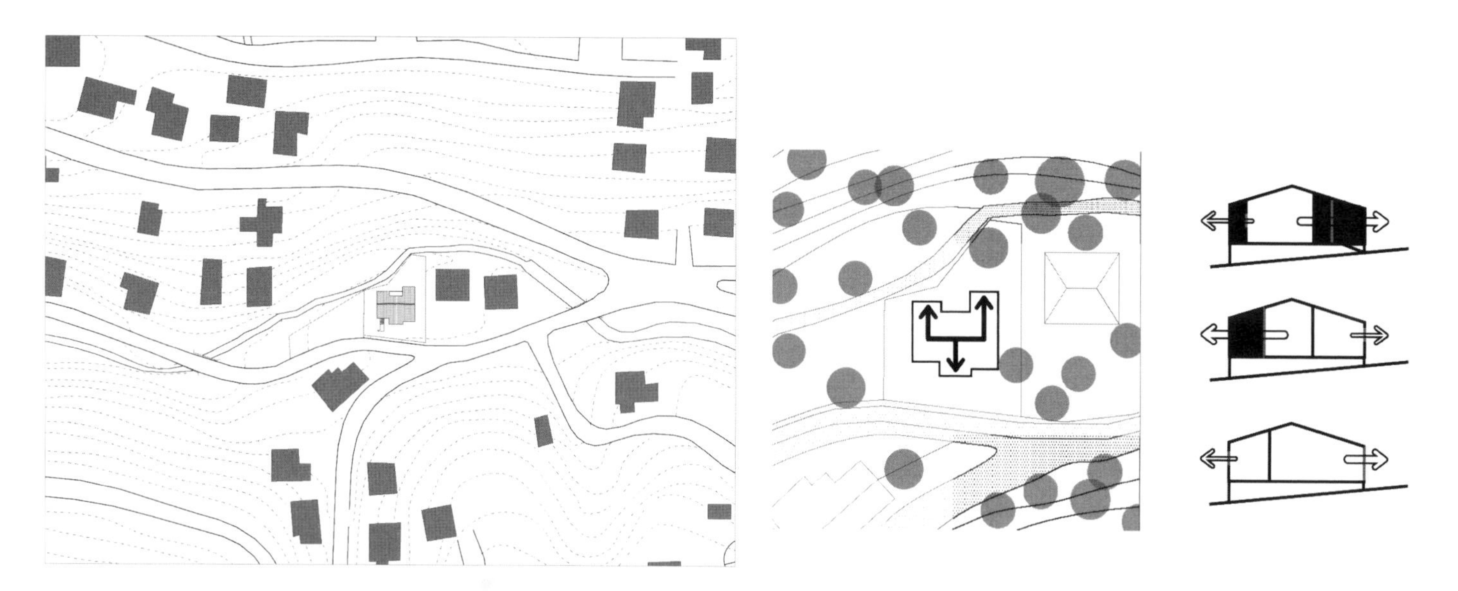

Playing with the simple saddleback-roof structure created an open interior space with a variety of light qualities, volumes and views. In contrast to the exterior, which is characterized as a compact and tranquil object in a forest, inside one can fully enjoy the dynamism and interaction between the inner space and the surroundings.

Elevations

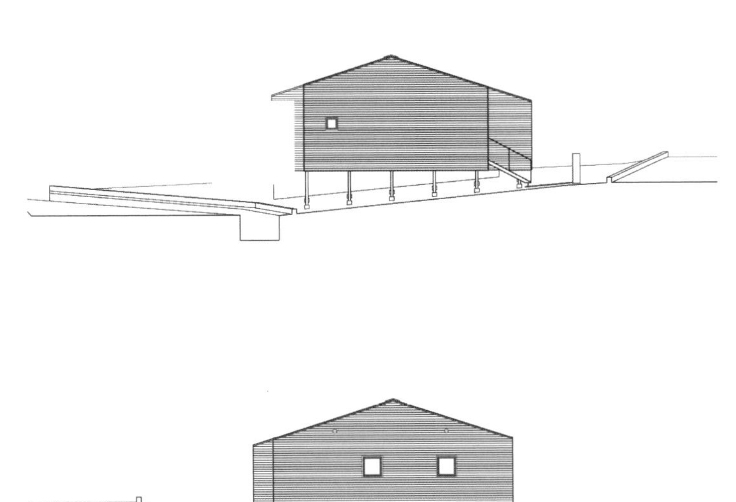

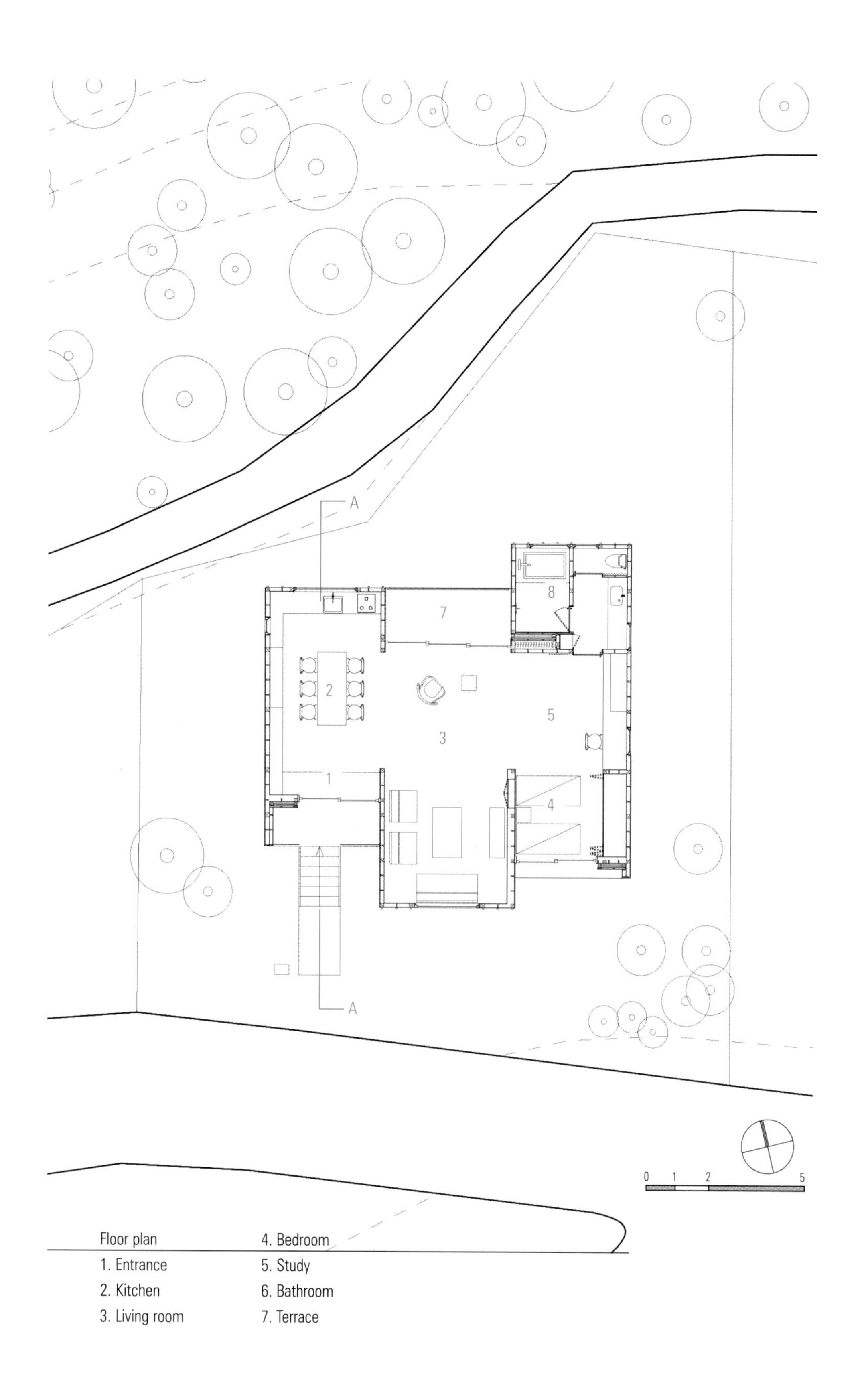

Floor plan

1. Entrance
2. Kitchen
3. Living room
4. Bedroom
5. Study
6. Bathroom
7. Terrace

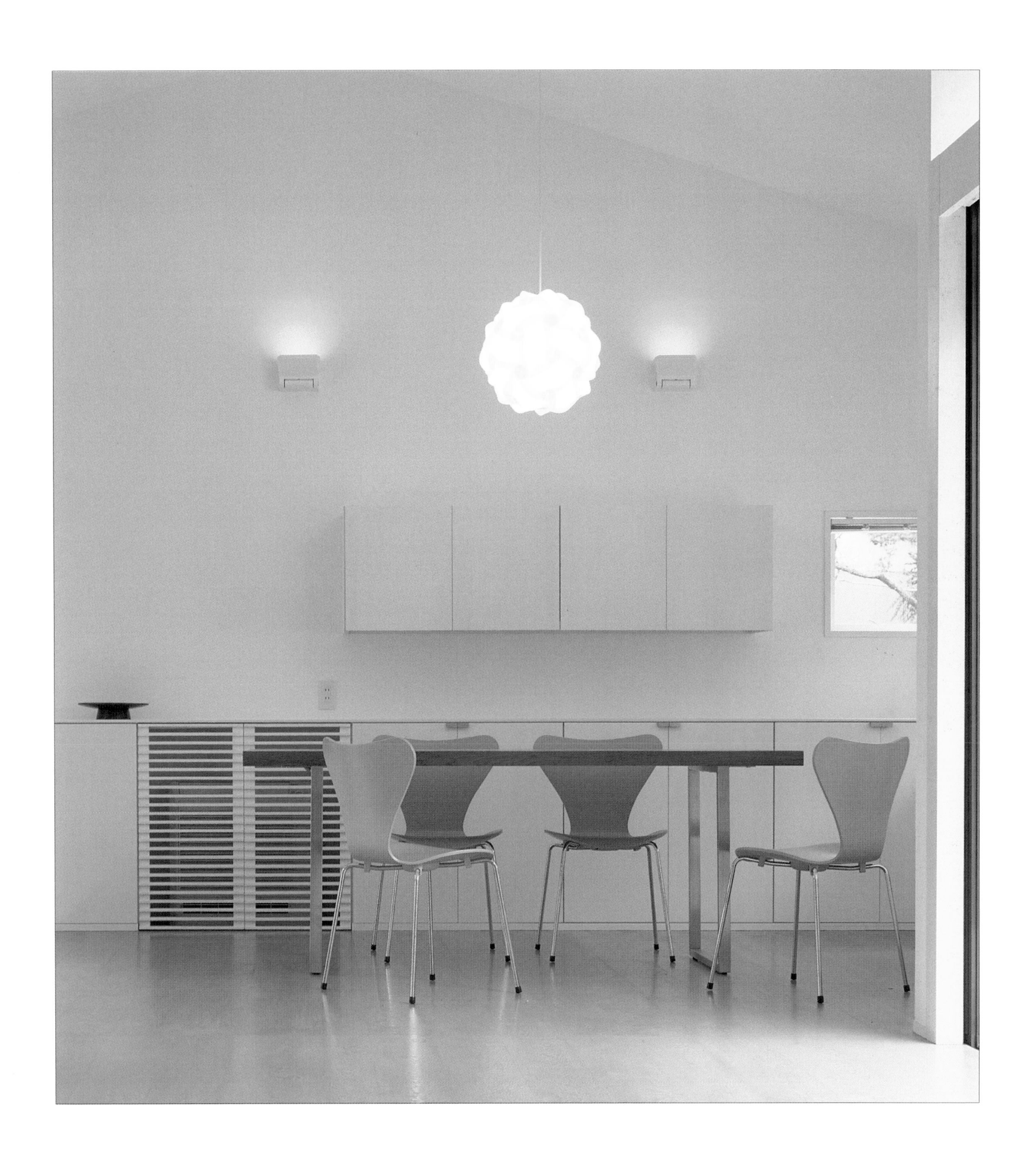

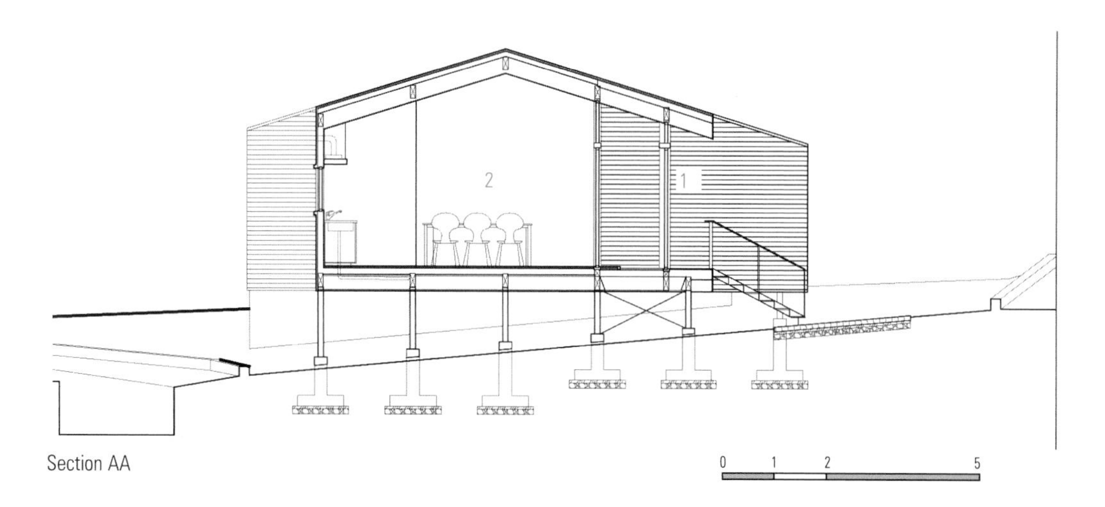

Section AA

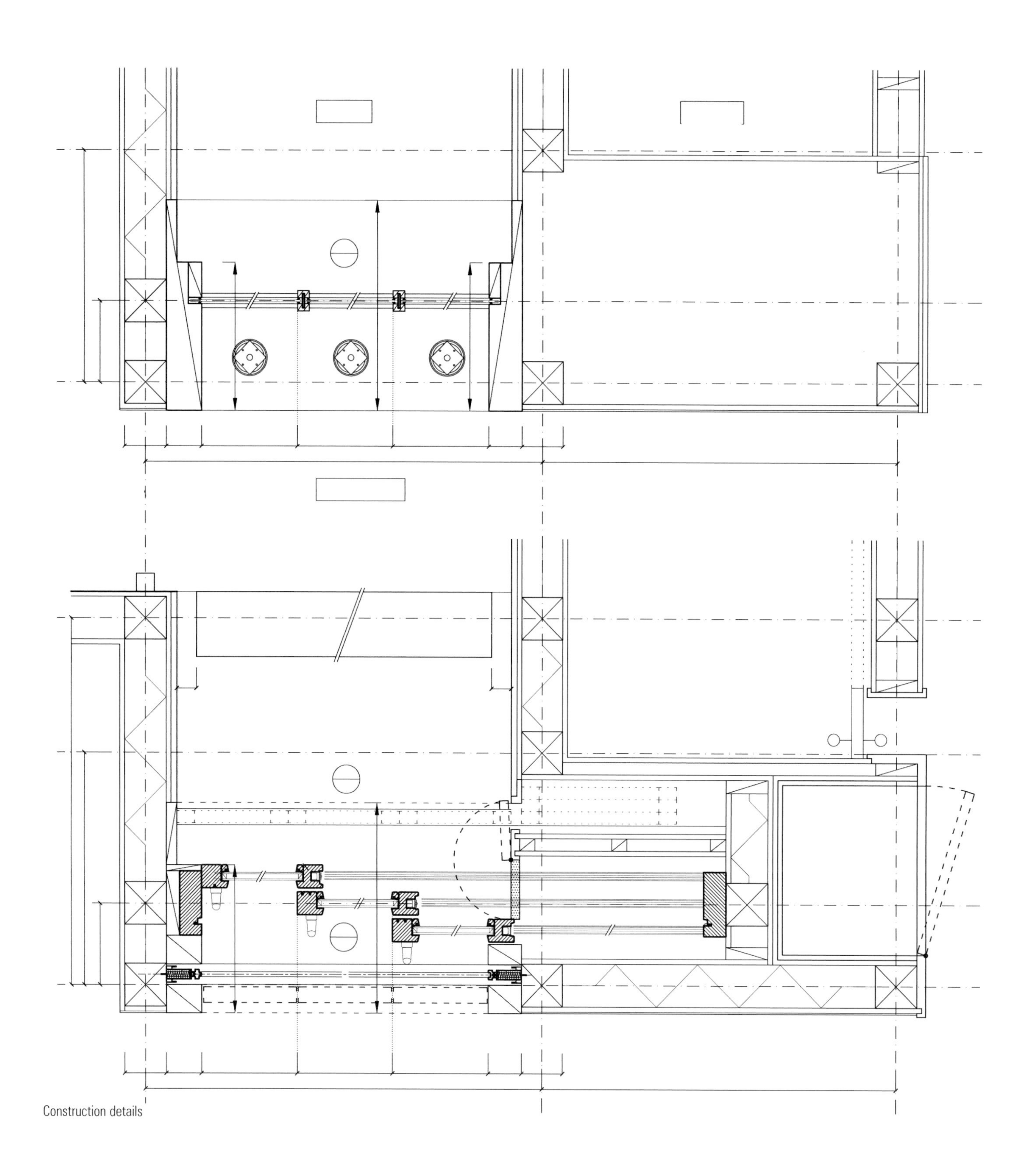

Construction details

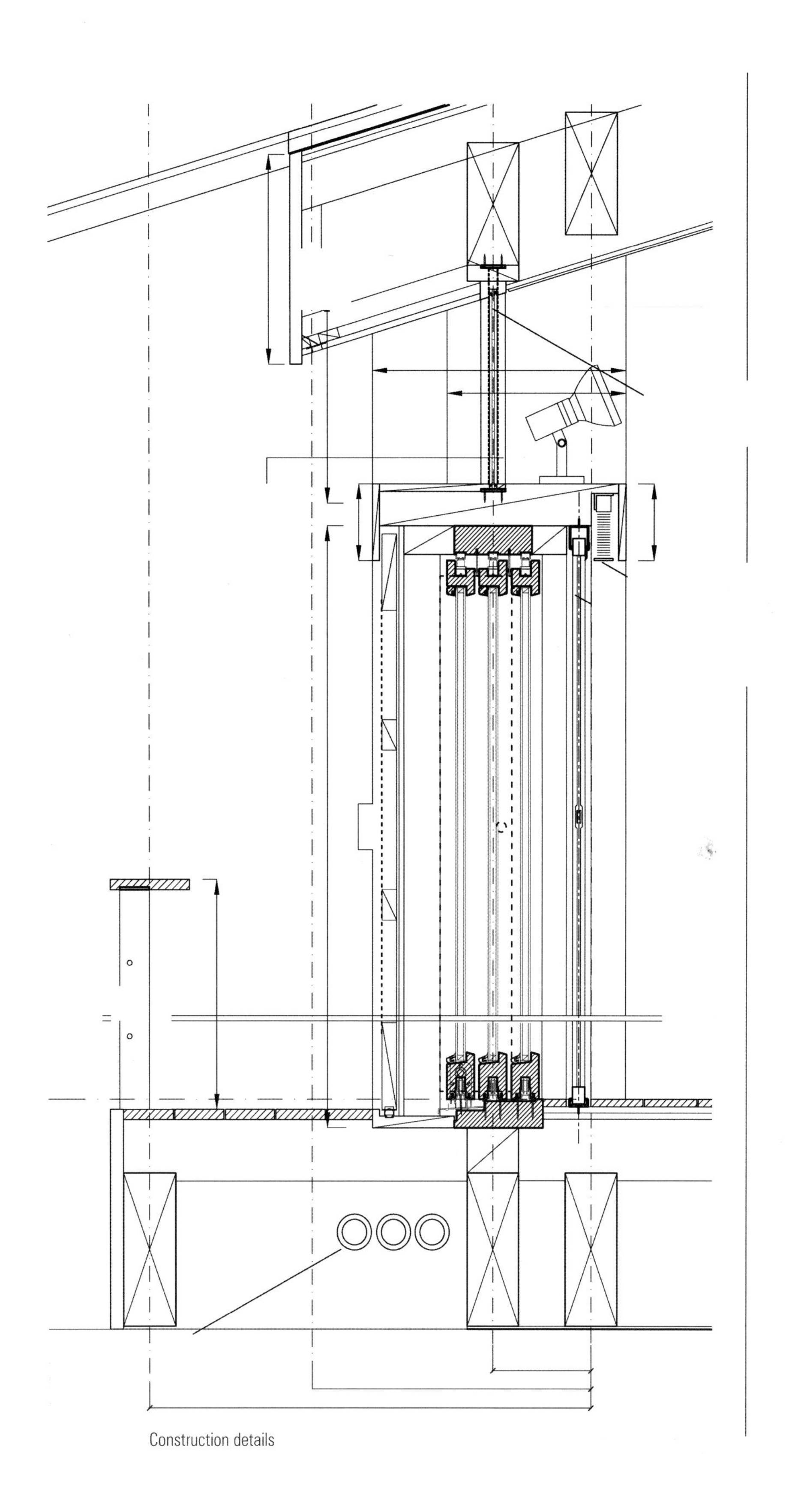

Construction details